IN A WORD

BOOKS BY MARGARET S. ERNST

Words: English Roots and How They Grow. *Knopf.*
Third edition, revised. 1954

More About Words. *Knopf. 1951*

IN A WORD

Text by MARGARET (Samuels) ERNST

Drawings by JAMES THURBER

Channel Press, Great Neck, New York

Printed in the United States of America

FOR

MORRIS (*dark*) LEOPOLD (*Lion of the people*)
ERNST (*serious*),

MY SERENDIPITY

preface by JAMES THURBER

THIS book was first published in 1939, the year all hell broke loose, and since then words, like everything else, have taken a bad tossing around. We seem to be entering what might be called an Oral Culture, at six hundred miles an hour, the modern American speed in most fields of activity and endeavor. It is an era of babble, on and off television and radio; and the written word, the word that enchants the eye instead of disturbing the ear, has sometimes seemed to me to be in danger of losing its shape and sense. There have been, to be sure, a few oral oases in the midst of the babble, such as Professor Bergan Evans' lively and devoted television program called "The Last Word," but the popularity of the offhand, unstudied interview has scarcely resulted in a service to our abused language.

In the past few years, having been alarmed by it all, I have written several pieces on behalf of sane usage, and against the shadow of formlessness that seems to have fallen upon both fiction and expository writing (formlessly called nonfiction) in our time and nation. It is, therefore, with high heart and hope that I join Margaret Ernst, that fond lover of the written word, in getting this special collection of words and drawings off to a new start and, I trust, a new audience.

The primary purpose of this compendium is to entertain, to fascinate, even to astonish word lovers, but it is my personal prayer that it will also serve to impress them with the importance of accurate speech, careful writing, and true meaning in a period of the world's history when those virtues of communication are becoming more and more essential to the security, such as it is, of Man on earth. No woman, for example, should call another woman "fastidious" unless she has looked up the meanings of that word and knows which one she has in mind. It is just possible that the other woman may know the word and never speak to her again.

The drawings that accompany some of these words are among the last that I was able to do in pen and ink before my sight began to dim in 1940. The illustration for "Candidate" was presented, twenty years ago, to Franklin Delano Roosevelt by his great friend, Morris Ernst, without, I am glad to say, disturbing their friendship in any way whatever. What became of that drawing I do not know, but what becomes of my drawings is, thank God, not one of the problems of our time, here or abroad.

In conclusion, I boldly seize this opportunity to explain, in answer to many questions, the meaning of the verb "to crevulate," which crept into a lighthearted dramatic study of confusion called *A Thurber Carnival*. Not even such a painstaking researcher as Mrs. Ernst could trace the origin of that verb beyond my own doorstep. It means, in the present participle "crevulating," the slight disturbance or complete collapse of everything from a summit conference to a wife's patience. I could not find, in any English dictionary, a word that seemed applicable to both of these unfortunate and menacing disintegrations.

West Cornwall,

Connecticut,

1960

contents

introduction

SINCE this book, now revised and enlarged, was first published in 1939 by Alfred Knopf, many factors in modern life have increased the reader's interest in words, their charm, their fun, the meaning that lies hidden in their individual histories. Every newspaper prints crossword puzzles, and the most unlikely people work them in the most unlikely places—jammed subways, for example. There are Double-crostics, Cryptograms, Scrabble, other word games, television programs asking questions about the meaning, use and origin of words. There are more and more books dealing with some phase of this subject, including my own *More About Words* and James Thurber's *The Wonderful O* and Theodore M. Bernstein's *Watch Your Language*.

Any amateur of words—in the literal French sense of lover—wants to know the story back of the syllables, how come so many words mean the opposite of what they once said (see *nice* or *silly* or *quaint*). This book puts between covers some of the many words I have found endearing or funny or exciting. With a little curiosity and a big dictionary you can do your own detective work.

Slang I do not scorn. Much slang is merely nonce-words, here today and gone tomorrow—*nonce* meaning for the one time only, from Middle English *then ones*—but often slang is poetic, picturesque and part of our tomorrow's speech. If it lives and fills a need, it finds a place in the dictionary eventually, as did *skyscraper* (see). Words are as full of changefulness and fickleness as an April sky; they are packed with the history of our mutable manners. A tart (feminine, non-edible) was once a sweetheart, and a candidate was a vote-getter trotting the streets of Rome in a white or *candid* toga. Many a fellow whose wife takes him laboriously through foreign art galleries and cathedrals considers travel hard work. How comforting to find that the history of language is with him—*travel* springs from the identic root as *travail*, because journeying, in the long ago, was full of toil and trouble.

We use words in a manner that fits contemporary thought and function. But back of almost every twentieth century accepted meaning is an earlier sense: more full of activity, less metaphoric, a literal picture of life in early Rome or Athens or in England, land of the Angles. When a Roman *insulted* some one, he *leaped* on him (or her) physically (Latin *in*, on; *salere*, leap or jump).

James Thurber, himself a magician with words, has illustrated this hidden and transigent meaning of many of the Apples of Gold. Study his drawings and you may find the key to the etymon, or true meaning, of language. Thereafter you will know when and if words are fitly spoken— "apples of gold in pictures of silver"; and you will have a fine time playing with words and their seductive ways. It is a game equally good in bathing-suit or best clothes; at a party or sailing in Nantucket Harbor; or even in bed.

My sources are too many to list, but if you want a few for your own explorations there are, to begin with, the *Oxford English Dictionary, An Etymological Dictionary of*

Modern English by Ernest Weekley, and H. L. Mencken's *The American Language.*

The index was generously compiled by a reader, Thomas K. Baker.

M. S. E.

New York, 1960

IN A WORD

" *A word fitly spoken is like apples of gold
in pictures of silver.*"

ABUNDANCE

A B C

Greek *Alpha Beta*, A B; Hebrew *aleph*, ox, and *beth*, house, from Phœnician symbols for letters. As simple as A B C. This word for our letters collectively was first used in the sixteenth century. The Old English alphabet had an extra letter called *thorn*. It represented our diphthong *th* and looked like this þ. When it was written with the loop open it made a Y, though it was still pronounced *th*. Hence the curse we now suffer from a plague of Ye Olde Shoppes.

abundance

Latin *ab*, from; and *unda*, wave. Nothing in nature seems more copious than the ocean, so we borrow, for our term for overflowing wealth, a picture of the waves. *Inundate* is, of course, a literal word for waves coming in or on. Ask the New England survivors of any great hurricane. *Superfluous* has almost the exact literal meaning of abundance; but whereas two's abundant, everyone knows three's a superfluity. In *affluence*, the flow is *toward* you. Generally used of money, but we suppose you could talk of an affluent tide and be correct.

achieve

French *venir à chef*, to come to a head. When you bring things to a head (even a boil), you have a sense of achievement, of accomplishment. *Mischief* meant, originally, the opposite of achieve — not to come to a head, but to grief. There was a Middle English word *bonchief*, meaning a good result. Recommended for revival.

admire

Latin *admirari*, to feel or express astonishment. There's not a hint in this word's early use to indicate what we now consider admiration. Here are some seventeenth-century appearances: " We may admire that so beastly a drunkard lived so long "; " Examples rather to be admired than imitated." A *miracle* is anything wonderful (same root: *mirus*, wonderful), as is a *marvel*.

aftermath

Old English *after;* and *mawan,* mowing. There is a
crop of grass which springs up after the first mowing
in the summer. When you cut it, you reap an aftermath. We don't know how the figurative aftermath
came, currently, to mean unpleasant consequences, unless the crop was wild oats? You can talk of a *later-
math* if you want a new (old) word.

alarm

Italian *all' arme,* Old French *alarme,* a call to (the)
arms. What was once upon a time a martial summons
to battle is now no more than a general feeling of
worry, and no less than a clock waking you hatefully
in the morning. Mr. Pepys (the older one — not
F. P. A.) wrote on July 14, 1665: " And so to bed, to
be up by times by the helpe of a larum watch." *Alert*
was the Italian *all' erta,* on the lookout, aloft.

alimony

Latin *alere*, to nourish. The original sense was that of feeding, operating the alimentary canal. Many gentlemen paying high alimony no doubt wish their ex-wives would study the derivation of the word and ask no more than food. Even caviar and champagne daily would seem cheap. The word in its present legal sense was used as long ago as 1655.

ambition

Latin *ambire*, to go about (for votes). A simple, naïve, and disarming word. And in spite of radio, newspapers, television and other twentieth-century extensions of the human voice, candidates (*see* candidate) still do go around asking for votes. You can be ambitious about many things not political, but a certain amount of going about is still entailed.

A L I M O N Y

arrive

Latin *ad*, to; *ripam*, shore; and *appellere*, to bring or come. Late Latin condensed these three words into one, *arribare*, meaning to bring or come to shore or into port. Strictly speaking, you can't arrive by train or car, but only by ship.

assassin

Arabian *hashsashin*, eaters of hashish. The original charter-member assassins were a religious sect in Palestine, Moslem fanatics, who were sworn by their Sheikh, the " Old Man of the Mountains," to murder all Crusaders. When fervor cooled, their leader gave them hashish to drink. Do modern Arabs still take a shot of hashish before shooting Jews? Marijuana is the same drug. We are not a crusader, but it gives us an uncomfortable feeling, just the same, to know that assassins still drink.

assets

French *assez*, enough; from the Latin *ad satis*, up to what is enough. According to Blount's very early Law Dictionary, assets were so called because they were sufficient " to discharge that burden, which is cast upon the heir, in satisfying the testator's debts or legacies." *Liabilities*, assets' twin, came from the Latin *ligare*, to tie or bind — you know, promissory notes, wives, children. From the same root: *liaison, league.*

astonish

Latin *extonare*, to strike by thunder. This word has become a great deal milder in the course of its history. An astonished person is more surprised than stunned. *Thunder* itself comes from the name of the Norse god Thor, the Thunderer. In the sixteenth century, a blow on the head *astonished* a man. Perhaps it still does today, though we'd say it knocked him cold. *Stun* was a Middle English word which meant to make a din.

ASTONISH

auburn

Old French *auborne*, Latin *alburnus*, whitish. Since this word meant originally flaxen, fair, how come it now means reddish brown? In the middle English dialect it became *abroune* and so became confused with *brown*. From Torriano's English-Italian Dictionary (1688): " that whitish colour of women's hair called an aburn colour." Platinum blond, we guess. From the same root: *alb*, a white priestly vestment; *albino; album*, originally a white tablet; *albumen*, white of egg.

auspicious

Latin *auspicium*, a watching of birds for the purpose of augury. The Roman *Augur*, the priest who foretold events, did so by watching the flight of birds. An auspicious occasion is one for which the birds fly right. Remember to watch the sparrows the next time you plan something. From the same roots: *aviary* (*auis* or *avis*, bird), *aviator, species, spy, spectator.*

AUSPICIOUS

ballot

Italian *balla*, ball. Secret voting in early days was done by dropping small balls in an urn or a box. Our present voting-machines have no resemblance to a ball at all, but the name sticks. *Bullet* is from the French form of ball, *boule*. Bullets and ballots are therefore the same — but not in a democracy, heaven be praised. The Venetians used bullets for drawing lots. To "blackball" was to drop in a ball of black, indicating a vote against a candidate.

bank

Old High German *banc*, bench, Italian, *banca*, money-changer's bench or table. In the old days bankers merely stood behind a wooden bench and did business — no bronze grilles, no vaults, no Greek temples. A sixteenth-century Bible has: "Christ overthrew the exchangers bankes." Most of our early financial words are Italian: *bankrupt*, originally *bankrout*, *banca rotta*, broken bench, now remodeled on Latin *rupta*, broken.

BALLOT

barbarous

Greek for foreign. An example of Attic hauteur and snobbery. Whoever came from other lands and couldn't speak Greek sounded to Athenian ears un-civilized, and their speech an unintelligible *bar-bar*. *Barbarism* meant originally the mixing of foreign words with Greek or Latin, and a *barbarian* was, in former days, not a Nazi but merely a poor guy who didn't talk classic Greek or Latin. What ho! the Barbary coast.

bastard

Old French, son of a pack-saddle. Someone not born legitimately in bed. Now a term of endearment. The word was widely used of William I, the Conqueror. The antique French also talked of a *coitrart*, son of a quilt, and the Germans of a *bänkling*, son of a bench. The English changed it to *bantling*. They all had a word for it.

BASTARD

bedizen

Anglo-Saxon *dīse*, a bunch of flax. In ancient times, you dizened — or bedizened — a distaff when you put flax on it ready for spinning. In other words, you decked it out, you dressed it up — but you had somewhere to go. Distaff was merely *dīse-stæf*, a bunch of flax on a staff.

bedlam

Middle English *Bedlam*, contraction of *Bethlehem*. The Hospital of St. Mary of Bethlehem, outside London, became a state lunatic asylum in 1547. Since then any row or behavior resembling the goings-on in a madhouse has been called bedlam. A similarly contracted word is *maudlin* from *Magdalen*. The sense of tearful comes from innumerable pictures showing Mary Magdalen repentant and weeping. *Tawdry* was *St. Audrey*, and the meaning grew from the shoddy necklaces and lace sold at St. Audrey's Fair.

belladonna

Italian, fair lady. But atropine to you, our oculist-visiting friend. The drug is made from deadly night-shade, the poison relative of decorative bitter-sweet. Those antique Italian gals knew a thing or two about expanding the pupil of the eye to give themselves lan-guorous glamour. Not everything was started by Elizabeth Arden.

bigot

Origin unknown, but there are some interesting spec-ulations and guesses as to where this word, looming so large in the color-divided world, came from. In a twelfth century French romance, *bigot* appears as the proper name of some people of South Gaul, and it has been suggested that it was an Old French version of Visigoth, "detestable foreigners or foreign heretics." Perhaps it was from Spanish *bigote,* moustache. The French applied the word in this sense, in the form *bigoz,* to the Normans, whose hairy faces they disliked.

binnacle

Middle English *bittacle*, Latin *habitaculum*, a small shelter. And so it is, very small. *Bilge* was merely an alteration of *bulge*, the place where a ship widened out in the hull and where foul water collected. *Starboard:* Anglo-Saxon *stēorbord*, steer board, the right side of the vessel, where the Viking or Early English steersman stood with his paddle. No wheel or tiller then. *Tiller* was originally the Old French for weaver's beam.

STARBOARD:
See Binnacle

biscuit

Latin *biscoctum*, twice baked. From the sixteenth to the eighteenth century it was spelled *bisket*. And it would be a help if it still were. The Oxford Dictionary defines a biscuit: " In U. S., a small, soft cake, usually fermented." Soft and a cake, indeed! They had better not say that below the Mason and Dixon line. Those are fighting words in Mississippi. There is a pottery biscuit, too, but that one is cooked only once. *Zwieback*, crunched by teething babies, is the German for twice baked.

blackmail

English *black;* and Scottish *mail*, rent or tribute. Small farmers in the north of England and along the Scottish border, in the old days, paid tribute to freebooter chiefs to gain immunity from plunder. This tribute was perhaps called *black* because it was often paid in black cattle. Rents paid in silver were called *white mail*.

bombastic

Greek, silkworm; Latin *bombax*, tree-silk (cotton), wadding. Figuratively, tall talk, well-stuffed boasting, padded with cotton or wool. *Farce* also means stuffing, from the Latin *farcire*, to stuff. So that's what's wrong with so many theatrical farces. In the eighteenth century housewives " farced " cucumbers, and even earlier they " bombasted " quilts.

book

Anglo-Saxon *bōc*, beech tree. Historians say the early English priests used smooth beech bark on which to scratch their runes. There was a Sanskrit word *bhurja* which meant birch bark for writing. *Paper* comes from *papyrus*, the Nile rush from which the first paper was made. And *parchment* from *Pergamum*, a city in Asia Minor where skin was first adopted as a substitute for papyrus.

boulevard

French, bulwark, rampart. As civilization emerged from the Dark Ages (or did it?), cities no longer needed their ramparts, their protecting walls. Instead of pulling them down, they used them as elevated promenades. *Avenue*, another French word, came from the Latin *ad venire*, to come to. An *adventure* is literally the same as an avenue — that which comes, what happens.

BOOK

bribe

Old French *bribe*, piece of bread. The etymologists put a ? after this derivation, but it is entertaining to think, if it is a true one, how bribes have increased in value. " A peece, lumpe, or cantill of bread, given unto a beggar," defines *bribe* in a dictionary of 1660, a reward not very acceptable today. The word is allied to *bribonis*, found in *Piers Plowman* as a synonym for vagabonds, rascals.

broker

Latin *broccare*, to broach or tap a cask. What a surprise for a Wall Street Dapper Don to find that historically he's a tapster who retails wine. Later the word came to mean any retail dealer, second-hand dealer, middleman. What the Germans call " luftmensch " — merchants of air. More ignominy for Wall Street: in 1694 a broker was a pimp and pander. Ben Jonson said: " One of the devils neere kinsmen, a broker "; and Heywood: " Two false knaves neede no broker."

BRIBE

buccaneer

Tupi (Brazilian) *boucan,* a gridiron. French hunters in Haiti and San Domingo smoked their wild-ox flesh over a boucan. Since these gentlemen were frequently pirates and free booters, they became *buccaneers,* in itself an innocent culinary word, meaning merely one who smokes meat over a grill. From Cotgrave's French-English Dictionary (1611): "*boucan:* a woodden-gridiron, whereon the cannibals broile pieces of men, and other flesh." Just a picnic.

budge

Latin *bullire,* to boil. Why is it that we never use this word in the positive sense? We say: "I won't budge from here," but never: "Budge along, give me room." *Budge* is used in *Hamlet* as a synonym for stir. Other words which we use only in a negative way: *inert,* never *ert; inept,* never *ept.*

B U D G E

budget

Latin *bulga*, a bag, wallet. Originally used in such expressions as " a budget of letters," " a budget of news." In Parliament the Chancellor of the Exchequer, in making his report, *opens his budget*, his brief-case. Hence our transfer of the name of the container to what is *in* the bag, estimated income and expense. *To budget* meant to put away in a wallet.

bunk, bunkum

American slang term. Coined from the name of a county in North Carolina, Buncombe, whose member in Congress once insisted on " making a speech for Buncombe." He wanted to be sure his constituents would know that he was doing things for them. Since that particular political gent, back in 1850, wasn't talking about anything, with no purpose but that of electioneering, we call any claptrap, tall talk, humbug: the bunk. A *bunk* to sleep in is something more honest. Probably from the Dutch *bank*, bench.

calculation

Latin *calx*, limestone; *calculus*, a pebble. When the human race progressed to counting more than twenty, beyond mathematical problems involving numbering the fingers and wiggling the toes, it used pebbles. So we go from the simplest system of reckoning to the most complex — differential calculus — in one word's etymology. The English word *chalk* comes from the same root.

calm

Greek, burning heat. At midday in Athens the air was very hot. Shops closed, athletes stopped throwing discuses, priests quit sacrificing, Greek choruses took naps — so we have our idea of calm as general rest in the world. There is a Provençal word *chaume*, meaning the time when the flocks rest.

calypso

The original *Calypso* was a sea nymph, queen of the Island of Ogyia, where Ulysses was wrecked and held for seven years. But there seems no connection between this lady and *calypso* as we hear it nowadays, that current-topics rhythmic ballad of Trinidad. Geoffrey Holder, a notable calypso singer, quotes Mr. Andrew Carr, president of the Trinidad Art Society, with this derivation: an African word *Kai-so*, meaning *Bravo;* or the French *carrousseaux*, a kind of formalized round-and-round parade, corrupted to *calliseaux*, *caliso* and eventually *calypso*.

campaign

Italian *campagna*, Latin *campus*, field. Originally this word meant open country. The military sense arises from the distinction between an army in the field and in quarters. *Champagne*, which scarcely makes you think of country scenes, takes its name from the French province of Champagne, meaning a rural district.

canary

Latin *canis*, a dog. The word *canary* no doubt means, to you, a bird, the color of the bird, a wine, or the islands from which all these get their names. But *canary* itself means pertaining to dogs, because what Roman navigators found remarkable about the Canary Islands was the huge wild dog population. Pliny mentions *Canaria insula*, isle abounding in large dogs.

cancan

Latin *quanquam*, although. This was the usual beginning of an erudite argument among university men. By a process of kidding, it came to mean first pedantic argument, then silly talk, finally — no one seems to know how — a bawdy dance of French origin. Doubtful etymology, but such fun — from Latinists to buttocks-wigglers.

CANARY

cancel

Latin *cancelli*, crossbars, lattice. When the postal clerk
cancels a stamp, he marks a lattice across it. When
you cancel a date, you mark it out with figurative crossbars. The *chancel* in a church was so called because of
the lattice separating the choir from the nave. A *chancellor* was originally the keeper of the bar at the en-
trance to a law court. Edward the Confessor made it
an official title.

candidate

Latin *candidatus*, white-robed. Among the Romans all
men seeking office had to wear white togas before elec-
tion day so that the voters might recognize them. Of
course they had no daily papers with candid-camera
shots, and no television; but even with them the white
toga mightn't be a bad idea. Presidential aspirants in
flowing robes, riding in an open car. *Candid* meant
white, fair, shining; hence, sincere. *Incandescent* is a
related word.

CANDIDATE

canopy

Greek, couch with mosquito bars or curtains. We still keep fairly close to the true meaning when we talk of a bed with a canopy, but when we speak of a hotel having a canopy over the sidewalk we are ludicrously remote from those Greek gnats. *Ludicrous:* Latin, pertaining to play.

canter

Short for *Canterbury pace*, the comfortable and leisurely speed at which the pilgrims used to jog along the Old Kent Road on their way to the shrine of Thomas à Becket at Canterbury Cathedral. See Chaucer. A critic of 1729 wrote: " The Pegasus of Pope, like a Kentish post-horse, is always on the Canterbury." *Canterbury bells*, flowers to you gardeners, were so called for their cupped resemblance to the bells jangling on the pilgrims' horses.

capricious

Latin *caprum,* of or belonging to a goat. We label
music written in a free fantastic style, and women's
whimsies, caprice — goat-like. Not very polite. However, this literal meaning is what the dictionaries so de-
lightfully term a nonce-use. The island of *Capri* was
once inhabited by goats. In fact you'd better be part
one yourself if you want to climb around it.

carnival

Latin *carnem levare,* to remove meat. Strictly speaking this word applies only to Shrove Tuesday (French
Mardi Gras — Fat Tuesday), the day before Lent be-
gins, and not to every firemen's celebration and riotous
festivity that comes along. Popular but mistaken etymology derives the word from Italian *carne,* flesh, and
vale, farewell. Carnival was changed by an *e* from a
time of fasting to a time of feasting. Related words are
carnal, relating to the flesh; *carnivorous,* meat-eating;
carnation, flesh-color; *incarnation,* in the flesh.

carouse

German *gar aus* (with *trinken* understood), to drink " all out." Sir Walter Raleigh, a knowledgeable man, wrote: "Some . . . garoused of his wine till they were reasonable pleasant." There is no relation between a *carousal* and a *carousel*. The prototype of those charming flying-horses in the park was the medieval tournament of knights on horseback or in chariots, and the word was, in Italian, *carosello*, little chariot.

C A R O U S E

cathedral

Greek, to sit down, seat. The *cathedra* is really the chair of a bishop in his church. *Cathedral* assumes the word *church* — the principal church of a diocese, housing the bishop's cathedra or throne; the episcopal *see*. *See* comes from the Latin *sedere*, to sit. When the medieval ranks *besieged* a fortress, they sat down before it and waited for the garrison to starve.

chagrin

French, from the Turkish *saghri*, rump of a horse, harsh leather; something that rubs you, or causes the skin to roughen as in goose-flesh. *Shagreen* (an English form of the same word) is a granular leather made from horse-skin. An eighteenth-century quotation: " Thoughts which . . . had made their skin run into a chagrin." Modern shagreen is usually shark-skin; modern chagrin still gives us prickly skin, or at least a red face.

chance

Late Latin *cadentia*, falling. Chance, then, is the way things fall for you, a word very applicable to a game of craps, for example. *Cadence*, from the same root, really means a falling voice or musical phrase. *Accident* means literally anything that happens or befalls, with no sense of disaster except by connotation. " A happy accident " is proper English.

chattel

Late Latin *capitale*, property, goods; literally, belonging to the head, *caput*. What the head owned chiefly was cattle. The Norman-Picard dialect made *cattle* of the Old French *chatel*, a corruption itself of the Latin word. " Shee is my goods, my chattels," occurs in *The Taming of the Shrew*. Have women ever enjoyed being cattle? We wonder if the twentieth-century lawyer, drawing up a chattel-mortgage, ever counts sheep jumping over a fence. *Capital offense* returns to the original Latin word *caput*, head. You lose it.

chauffeur

Colloquial French for fireman. Do you remember those steam-driven early motor cars? Chauffeur, or stoker, was a derisive nickname for motorists of 1900. *Automobile* means self-moving, from the Greek.

CHATTEL

cheater

Middle English *escheatour*, one who looked after escheats: under feudal law, reversion of property to the lord when the tenant died without an heir. This legal word has come down in the world in this way: (1) a cheater (escheator), an officer who attended to escheats; (2) a dishonest escheator — there must have been plenty; (3) any dishonest person.

chivalry

Latin *caballarius*, horseman, cavalier. To treat a lady chivalrously is to treat her as a medieval knight would. We doubt very much if she'd like it. Related words, all having to do with horses and horsemen: *cavalry*, *chevalier*, *cavalcade*, which meant a mounted raid. Such manufactured words as *motorcade* and *Aquacade* have no meaning at all.

cigar

Spanish *cigarra*, cicada. Because a cigar was supposed to resemble the dark cylindrical body of a locust. French *cigarette*, little cigar. This is " popular etymology," not scholarly and authentic.

cinch

Spanish *cincha*, cingle. The saddle-girth used in Mexico and Spain, holding the saddle tightly to the horse or burro. Hence our slang term *to cinch*, meaning to make sure, tight. " It's a cinch " — it's sure, in the bag.

civilization

Latin *civilis*, of or pertaining to people in cities. A word to make farmers, foresters, and country gentlemen froth at the mouth. The snobs of Rome went further. A *savage* was a person who lived in the woods (Latin *silva*, wood, *silvaticus;* Old French *salvage*). See *urbane*.

client

Latin *cluere*, to listen to. A heyday for lawyers, and how true. Originally this word was used to mean a dependent; then, in France, a customer. The word *client* appears in 1306 in the Year-books of Edward I. " Good Counsellors lacke no Clients," says Shakespeare in *Measure for Measure*.

CIVILIZATION

climate

Greek, slope. Early meteorologists meant by climate the slope from the equator to the poles; in other words, a region of the earth. Later, climate came to mean the atmosphere and temperature of that region. Now a synonym (in ad-writers' blurbs) for Florida, southern California, Italy, et al. We are not sure they admit we have a climate in New York.

climax

Greek, ladder. A very precise and nice picture-word of ideas or events rising rung by rung to the uppermost step. Properly speaking, the climax is the act of rising, not the top reached after the climb. *Anti-climax* is like the Greek *bathos*, depth. Hand us the step-climax, please.

Cockney

Middle English *coken-ey*, cock's egg. To go from an egg to a Londoner of certain characteristics, Cockney traveled so: at first it was one of the small abnormal eggs hens sometimes lay, called " cocks' eggs "; next it was used for a " child that sucketh long," a milksop; then, contemptuously, for any townsman; finally, for a Londoner. In *Piers Plowman* we find: " I have no salt Bacon, Ne no Cockeneyes, bi Crist, Colopus to maken."

companion

Latin *com-*, together; and *panis*, bread. Those who broke bread together and were, therefore, mates, fellows. You didn't eat with a man and then knife him. Nowadays this nicety isn't always observed. When you have *company* for dinner, you are talking literally of the rolls you'll share. A *pantry* was a place where bread was made or kept. The Sanskrit word for nourish was *pā*. *Appanage* comes from the same root, meaning, literally, to supply with bread.

compunction

Latin *com-*, with; and *pungere*, to prick. When you feel compunction for an ill deed done, you are pricked or stung by conscience. See *remorse*. A *pungent* taste or smell pricks your tongue or your nose; and pungent speech stings your mind. To *punctuate* is to mark with points or pricks; a *puncture* in your tire is a prick; to be *punctual* is to be on the dot or prick; and to be *punctilious* is to pay attention to fine points.

conciliate

Latin *concilium*, council. Behind the current idea of gaining goodwill is an honester historical meaning — a coming together in council for discussion, an evaporation of differences through meeting. A *reconciliation* is a meeting again (Latin *re-*) after differences.

COMPUNCTION

congregation

Latin *con-*, together; and *grex, greg-*, herd. So we sit
in churches and lecture-halls, as woolly, warm, and
contented as a flock of sheep. The one who feeds us is
our *pastor*, a shepherd, from the Latin *pascere*, to feed.
Pasture is a related word. The *egregious* man is the
one who is chosen out of the flock: Latin *ē*, out of;
grege, the flock. Originally, not a disparagement.
Those of us who are *gregarious* are birds of a feather.
We flock together.

constable

Latin *comes stabuli*, count of the stable. This high dignitary of the Roman Empire has now become the nadir
of officialdom. A *marshal* was Old High German for
horse-servant; a *steward* Anglo-Saxon for sty-ward or
keeper of the pigs. Ancestry of the royal house of
Scotland — the Stewarts and the Stuarts.

cosmetics

Greek *kosmos,* order, ornament. Pythagoras called the world or universe *kosmos* from its perfect order and arrangement. (A good thing he can't see it today.) And from this planetary idea we come down to modern woman's *cosmetics,* on which the American sisters spend hundreds of millions a year. From *kosmos* meaning order, the Greeks derived *kosmein,* to put in order, and then *kosmetikos,* skilled in arranging or adorning. Cosmetics have been used since history began. The ancient Egyptian beauties used *kohl* to shadow their eyes. *Kohl* is an Arabic word for a powder made of finely crushed antimony. You see it smudged thickly around the eyes of tiny boys in India. *Mascara* has the same derivation as *masquerade,* which it is when girls use it too freely: Spanish *mascara,* a mask, from the Arabic *maskhara,* laughing-stock, buffoon. Be careful with your makeup, ladies, or you'll look like a clown. *Mask* is a related word. A *cosmocrat* is lord or ruler of the world; *cosmophil* means friendly to the world in general; and the *cosmos* in your garden, pink or white, is a round world-shaped flower.

courtesan

Italian *cortigiano*, a courtier. One attached to the court of a prince, man or woman. Perhaps the ladies of the court were no better than they should be. At any rate, the word soon came to mean a woman attached to the court for a very specialized purpose. " Your whore is for every rascall, but your Curtizan is for your Courtier," says a seventeenth-century commentator. *Courtesy* was court manners, and so was *curtsy*. *Tart* (feminine, not pastry) is a shortening of *sweetheart*.

crescent

Latin *crescere*, to grow. There is nothing in the word *crescent* to indicate new-moon-shaped. But since the *crescent* moon meant the growing or waxing moon, English transferred the lunar shape to the adjective. You could say, logically, " a crescent figure," " a crescent boy," or " a crescent debt."

COURTESAN

crestfallen

Latin *crista*, tuft, plume; and Old English *feallen*, to fall. This hybrid compound is borrowed from the ancient and modern sport of cock-fighting. The rooster with his crest drooping is the licked one in a fight. And the same pathetic picture was true of a knight defeated, his plumed helmet trailing the ground.

curfew

Old French *couvre-feu*, cover the fire. At a certain early hour of the evening a bell rang — you put out your fire and went to bed. " Well, 'tis nine o'clock, 'tis time to ring curfew," says an author, *circa* 1608. Early to bed and early to rise — but almost no one was healthy, wealthy, or wise.

cynic

Greek, a dog. Because the characteristic expression of a cynic is like that of a surly dog. Since the cynics of Greece sneered at wealth and ease and fun, they were dogs-in-the-manger. *Cynosure:* Greek for dog's tail, the center of attraction. Milton wrote of "Some beauty . . . the cynosure of neighbouring eyes." Not very complimentary. Cynosure is another name for the constellation Ursa Minor, in whose bear's tail is the Pole-star.

days of the week

Monday, Anglo-Saxon *mōnandæg,* moon day. *Tuesday, Tiwesdæg,* day of *Tiw,* a Teutonic god identified with the Roman Mars, though the word is cognate with the Greek Zeus. *Wednesday, Wodnesdæg,* day of Woden or Odin. *Thursday, Thunresdæg,* day of Thor the Thunderer. *Friday, Frigedæg,* day of Frigg, wife of Odin, Norse goddess of love. From the same root as *free, friend* (which see). *Saturday, Sæternesdæg,* an Anglo-Saxon translation of the Latin *Saturni dies,* day of Saturn. *Sunday, sunnandæg,* the sun's day.

debate

Latin *de*, down; and *battere*, to fight, to beat. A debate was never meant to be a polite affair such as goes on in college debating societies. The hockey-stick emphasis of an argument at Madison Square Garden, between the Rangers and *Les Canadiens*, carries the true idea of a debate — you beat down your opponent. *Discuss* is another violent bit of verbiage from the Latin: *dis-*, apart; and *quatere*, to shake.

deliberate

Latin *de*, thoroughly; and *librare*, to balance or weigh. *Libra* were scales. A cerebral expression for what was once a physical act. *Ponder*, a strict synonym for deliberate, came from the Latin *pondus*, weight. *Preponderance* is the act of outweighing.

DEBATE

delirium

Latin *de*, away from; and *lira*, ridge or furrow. A fine old farmer's way of talking about plowing a crooked furrow. When the oxen strayed, they were delirious. Tremens? Only if they trembled too. They say Boston's streets were laid out by cows in delirium.

derivation

Latin *de*, from; and *rivus*, river. This " derived from " stuff running through IN A WORD is just Ol' Man River, after all. Literally, this word *derivation* means the leading of a current of water from a source to another part; figuratively, it means tracing a word to the source from which it flows. See *arrive*.

derrick

Dutch *Dirk* or *Dierryk,* a proper name meaning mighty people. About 1600, at Tyburn Prison in London, there was a hangman whose surname was Derrick. He did his suspensory work so famously and so copiously that his name has passed over into the language to denote, first, the gallows; and latterly, any contrivance for hoisting.

dexterity

Latin *dextra*, the right hand. In this right-handed race, everything adroit is called dexterous, while left-handed acts are branded *sinister*, from the Latin word for the left hand, *sinistra*. Most unfair, when you consider that about one-third of our population is left-handed. The popularity of south-paws is changing things. The French word for left is *gauche* (our *gawky*); and their *droit*, right, has come to mean *the Law*. There's the left-handed compliment, the left-handed marriage — the hand actually used in morganatic ceremonies — and the favored right-hand man. Also the *Left* in politics — a threat.

DEXTERITY

dicker

Latin *decuria*, a set of ten, especially ten hides. The Anglo-Saxons made the word into *dicer*. It is used in the Domesday Book and is said to refer to the ten hides which Cæsar's soldiers in Britain adopted as their unit of barter. Frontiersmen in America used *dicker* when they bartered for skins with the Indians.

diplomat

Greek, a doubling. A vivid word-picture of what goes on in diplomatic circles. Everything the career boys do is like a *diploma* (in its original form) — folded over twice — so you can't see what's underneath. "An ambassador is an honest man sent to lie abroad for the good of his country," wrote Sir Henry Wotton. Our quotation doesn't specify *how* lie. Perhaps he meant sex in diplomacy. *Duplicity* is a related word from a Latin root meaning double or two-timing.

disaster

Latin *dis-*, against, away from; and *astra*, stars. If you disregard your horoscope — play the market on Tuesday when the astrologers say Thursday, for example — you are courting *disaster*. Someone in 1635 defined a disaster as "an obnoxious planet." *Ill-starred* has the same sense of unlucky. In botany, an *aster* is star-shaped. And in printing, an *asterisk*.

easel

Dutch *ezel*, German *esel*, ass. A patient creature, an easel, standing quietly as his beast of burden while an artist paints. The kind you buy in art stores doesn't even require feeding and currying. The French word for easel is *chevalet*, little horse. Many of our painting terms are borrowed from the Dutch — *landscape* (shape of land), and *lay figure* (figure with pliant limbs).

E A S E L

economy

Greek *oikos*, house; and *némein*, manage. The wife who talks of economizing is using the word in its original sense; but a college professor who gives a course in political economy must be speaking figuratively of the household management by citizens collectively, the state being their house. An *economist* is — or ought to be — a house-keeper. When you talk of *domestic economy* you are guilty of tautology — it means house management. *Domestic* comes from the Latin *domus*, house or home.

ecstasy

Greek, displacement. In ecstasy, whether from passion, pain, fear, or astonishment, you lose your mind — there is a displacement. The word came later to mean a trance, a frenzy, catalepsy. Nowadays most people think of ecstasy as an extreme but pleasurable emotion, rapture. The phrase " to be beside oneself " is another way of saying you're ecstatic.

E C S T A S Y

electricity

Greek, amber. Have you ever rubbed a bead of amber on wool and tested its electrical power of picking up bits of paper? Our word for this power was coined from the Greek name of amber. We doubt if this poetic etymology cheers up the chief actor in an *electrocution*. The word *electrocution* was coined in 1889 by fusing *electro-* with the rear end of *execution* (Latin *ex*, out; and *sequi*, follow).

eliminate

Latin *ex*, out; and *limen*, threshold. To eliminate something, you put it out of doors. Before you go to bed, put out the light and eliminate the cat. A *sublime* idea is one raised up to the lintel; and *subliminal* is a psychological word coined to designate things below the threshold of sensation or consciousness.

ELIMINATE

emancipation

Latin *e*, away; *manus*, hand; and *capere*, take. Literally, when Lincoln issued the Emancipation Proclamation, he told the slave-owner to take away his hand. *Manufacture* meant to make by hand; *maneuver*, work with the hands; *mandate*, to give by hand; and a *manacle*, that police jewelry, was a Roman lady's sleeve. In Old English, *handsome* meant merely handy, quick with the hands.

emotion

Latin *emovere*, to move away or much. A very good literal description of what a feeling of affection does to you. We say: "She was in a *transport* [literally, carried across] of joy." *Enraptured* is from the Latin *rapere*, to snatch. Originally, *rapt* meant carried up to heaven like Elijah. *Rape* comes from the same root, but has little traffic nowadays with heaven. *Ravish*, also akin, has two meanings, too. You can be ravished, carried away, by music; or by men. The latter has implications. *Rapacious* persons are snatchers, and so are *rapids* in a river.

enchant

Latin *incantare*, sing. The Sirens and other mythological ladies sang to the victims they wanted to vamp. In Latin *carmen* meant song, incantation. It is from this root that we get our word *charm*. Yet people with charm, people who enchant us, frequently can't sing a note.

enemy

Latin *in-*, not; and *amicus*, friend. All very clear and precise. From the same source: *amicable, inimical*. Going further back along the same root we have the Latin *amare*, to love, with *amiable, amity, amorous*, as derivatives.

enthrall

French *en*, in; and Middle English *ral*, a thrall, serf, slave, runner. When you are enthralled by a person, a play, a scene, you are enslaved. See *enchant*.

enthusiasm

Greek, possessed by a god. If you talk of being enthusiastic about football or crêpes suzettes — and who doesn't? — you are exaggerating.

ENTHRALL

Latin *e*, from; and *rudis*, rude. The erudite man is one freed from rudeness. Originally the word was used in the literal sense of cultivation, in pruning trees, lopping off dead or asymmetrical branches. Latin *raudus* meant rough red iron ore, unrefined. A *rudiment* is something in the rough, a first attempt.

escape

Late Latin *ex*, out of; and *cappa*, cape or cloak. Flee-
ing, you get away so narrowly that you leave your
cloak behind in the pursuer's hands. A true picture-
word. An *escapade* generally ends up without a wrap
too. The Roman capes must have had hoods, because
capa meant hood, something worn on the *caput*, head.
The liberty cap is the Phrygian head-dress given to
Roman slaves as a token of emancipation.

excruciating

Latin *crucem*, cross. When we describe a play as
excruciatingly funny we are using too fierce and serious
a word. *Excruciating* literally means to *crucify*, to
torture. Figuratively, it means to cause extreme mental
pain or anguish. However, the expression came into
use hyperbolically, humorously, in the nineteenth
century. Dickens, in *Nicholas Nickleby*, wrote: "Why
is she so excruciatingly beautiful?" Related words are
crucifer, cross-bearer, *crucial*, supreme trial or choice,
cruciform, cross-shaped as are certain flowers, and
crux, as in "the crux of the matter."

exhilarate

Latin *ex*, create state of; and *hilaris*, cheerful. If you say mountain air exhilarates you, you mean the purer oxygen makes you physiologically more cheerful. If you say champagne exhilarates you, you are no doubt literal and honest, though Samuel Johnson said: " No, Sir; wine gives not light, gay, ideal hilarity; but tumultuous, noisy, clamorous merriment." An old sourpuss. *Hilarious* derives from the same root, as does the proper name *Hilary*. Hilarius, Bishop of Poitiers, who died in 367, has a festival celebrated annually on January 13th.

expedite

Latin *ex*, out; and *pes*, the foot. Literally, to free or extricate the foot — no doubt in order to run or kick. Following the idea, an act is *expedient* if you're foot-loose and fancy-free at the moment. To be *impeded* is to put your foot in it. When it comes to an *impedi-ment* in speech, our metaphor is badly tangled. Every time you open your mouth you put your foot in it.

exquisite

Latin *ex*, out; and *quærere*, to seek. An exquisite girl, flower, sunset, line of poetry — is one sought out, not a run-of-the-mill girl, flower, sunset, line. The French *recherché* means the same. Shakespeare used the word in its exact sense when he wrote: " I have no exquisite reason for't, but I have reason good enough." There used to be a verb *exquire*, to seek out, just as there is *inquire*, to seek into.

fastidious

Latin *fastidium*, loathing. J. T. is quite correct in his Preface when he says that no woman should call another "fastidious." It does *not* mean dainty or over-neat or careful about your grooming or choosy about your food, though most people use it in these ways. Originally, *fastidious* was that which creates disgust, disagreeable, distasteful; then it changed roles and became the person disgusted, hence disdainful, scornful, full of pride; and finally squeamish, over-nice, hard to please. A sixteenth century work speaks of "A fastidious Ulcer." The dictionary grants it no complimentary use, ever.

fee

Anglo-Saxon *feoh*, cattle. Since in those days cattle represented a man's wealth, *fee* came to mean money. We would like to see our favorite attorney's face if a client paid his fee literally. A fine sight to see a drove of Jersey cows going up in the elevator at 285 Madison. See *impecunious* for a similar Latin derivation, and *chattel* for French. The *feudal* system (a word from the same root) was based on wealth, property.

FEE

filibuster

Dutch *vrijbuiter*, freebooter. Those members of Congress who talk for days in order to obstruct legislation are, in short, nothing more than freebooters. The original freebooters were piratical adventurers engaged in plundering West Indian colonies.

flotsam

French *flotter*, to float. Flotsam's inseparable twin, *jetsam*, came from the Old French *jeter*, to throw. So flotsam and jetsam, whether in the ocean or in society, is that which floats and is cast up. Cowell in 1637 in his *Interpreter* (the first edition was condemned by Parliament and burnt by the hangman) wrote: " *Flotson*, alias *flotzam*, is a word proper to the seas, signifying any goods that by shipw[r]acke be lost, and bye floting, or swimming upon the top of the water, which with *jetson* and *lagan* be given to the Lord Admirall." *Lagan* was what lay on the bottom. *Jettison* is a related word; also *jetty*. Maybe we need a new word for what's thrown out of rockets—*orbitage?*

FILIBUSTER

focus

Latin, hearth, fireplace. In the days before we became nomads of the apartment-house era, the hearth was the *focus* of the home and home life. Now, like poor photography, we are out of focus. The word was first used in a mathematical sense in 1604 by Kepler, who likened the *focus* of a curve to the burning-point of a lens.

fog

Norwegian *fogg*, long, coarse, dry grass, left standing through the winter. The word also meant moss, gray, clinging; and a poetic language then transferred it to gray and clinging mist. As a verb, *to fog* meant variously: to become overgrown with moss, to leave long grass uncut, to feed cattle on this grass. *Foggy* meant marshy, boggy, moss-grown; hence our *fogy* or *fogey*, an insult usually preceded by " old."

fool

Latin *follis*, bellows, wind-bag, also scrotum. It seems
no woman can really be a fool! The Latin plural *folles*
meant puffed cheeks, whence the term was transferred
to a jester. Early paper-makers employed the cap and
bells of a fool as a watermark — hence foolscap paper.
Fop was originally *fool*.

friend

Anglo-Saxon *freond*, to love. *Freo*, not in bondage, gave us our *free*. So we have the early English idea of free love — in friendship there are no bonds, no shackles. Members of the Early English family, not thralls born in serfdom, were loved, and therefore *free*.

FRIEND

galaxy

Greek, milk. A brilliant crowd of beautiful women and distinguished men, generally used by society editors to describe the opening of the opera season, means nothing more nor less than white fluid Vitamin D, fine for babies. The Greek astronomers used this simple word for the Milky Way; and the sixteenth-century poets likened a glowing assemblage to that luminous band of stars circling the heavens. The Latin-born word *lacteal*, relating to milk, is akin.

GALAXY

gerrymander

American journalese, nineteenth century. Elbridge
Gerry, Governor of Massachusetts, ingeniously started
the system of faking electoral districts by reshaping
them. One such renovated district looked like a sala-
mander, and a smart journalist combined the Governor's name with that of the lizard to form *gerry-
mander*.

gospel

Old English *godspel*, good story. *Spell* was the Anglo-
Saxon word for saying, narrative, set of words, magic
formula. Gospel at first meant any rousing tale. Only
later, popular etymology made the " good " into
" god " and borrowed the word to mean God's story,
or the life of Jesus.

gossamer

Middle English *gosesomer*, goose summer. The time of year when it is open season for eating geese and when *gossamer* is seen. You may have thought *gossamer* just an adjective for describing nylon evening stockings, but it's actually those fine-spun spider-webs you see traced on the grass and shrubbery in lovely autumn weather. November 11th, St. Martin's, seems to have been the big goose-eating day in England.

gossip

Anglo-Saxon *godsibb*, god-relative, kindred in God. The old sense was that of a sponsor in baptism. By Shakespeare's day the meaning of crony, idle chatterer, had become attached — presumably because two women, acting as godmothers at a baptism, naturally *gossiped* together over the event, with or without benefit of clergy. The attribute by now is not exclusively feminine.

GOSSIP

govern

Greek, to steer a ship. When we elected Skipper
Roosevelt to take our helm, the voters must have been
reading the dictionary. The Ship of State is a figure of
speech growing logically from *govern*. In sixteenth-
century England a rudder was a *governail,* and a pilot
or captain a *governor.*

gringo

Mexican Spanish. A contemptuous term for Americans, said to be derived from the fact that the Americans were eternally singing a song about " Green grow
the rushes, oh." Green grow – *gringo.* Not authenti-
cated, but such a lovely story. Dates from 1884.

grocer

Medieval Latin *grossus*, gross. Originally, one who bought or sold in the gross, a wholesale merchant or dealer. In popular meaning this word has completely reversed itself. Nowadays a grocer is not a wholesaler unless you specifically say so. Grocers in the Middle Ages dealt in spices, sugar, and other foreign produce, just as the Great Atlantic and Pacific Tea Company (A. & P. to you) brought home tea in its clipper ships.

grog

English slang, about 1770. There was an Admiral Vernon in the British navy who habitually wore a *grogram* cloak. His sailors nicknamed him " Grog " from the cloth, and none too lovingly, since it was he who first ordered dilution of sailors' rum. Naturally, the watered liquor became *grog* too; and an unsteady gait, *groggy*. A red nose is a *grog-blossom*.

guillotine

French *Guillotin*, the name of a physician who, in 1789, suggested the use of the swift and tidy guillotine in place of earlier and sloppier methods of beheading. In 1883 in the United States the dismissal of Government officials on the coming in of a new President was called guillotining. A sort of purge.

GUILLOTINE

halcyon

Greek kingfisher, from *sea* and *conceiving*, because of the belief that the bird hatched its young in a floating nest during the *halcyon* days. The Greeks believed that the bird charmed the wind and waves into quietude. Hence, calm, undisturbed, became synonymous with *halcyon*.

HALCYON

halibut

Middle English *halybutte*, holy butt. A butt was a flat fish commonly eaten on fast or holy days. We doubt if Fulton Fish Market knows this bit of word-history. There is no taint of holiness in its language. The word *holy* itself derives from Old English *hál*, whole or hale — anything holy is kept inviolate, intact.

handicap

English *hand in cap*, a lottery game in which lots were drawn from a cap. Samuel Pepys, on September 19, 1660, wrote: " Among the pleasures some of us fell to handycapp, a sport that I never knew before." As early as *Piers Plowman* the game was described. It seems that it was a custom to barter articles, and to give odds with the inferior article, as settled by an umpire. All the players put forfeit-money in a cap. The name refers to the drawing-out of full or empty hands, to settle whether the match was accepted or not. From there we got to horse-racing, with a referee deciding what weight the favorite was to carry, and the owners drawing from a cap to declare the race on or off.

handkerchief

Anglo-Saxon *hand*, hand; and French *couvre chef*, cover the head. At first we had a *kerchief* for covering the head (see current ads of women's accessories), then we carried a head-covering in the hand, and finally we put it in a pocket — pocket-handkerchief. See *achieve*.

harangue

Old High German *hring*, ring, circle of audience. This word has come to mean the ranting oration of a speaker, but where would your soap-box fellow be without his circle of listeners in Union Square or at Hyde Park Corner? No one harangues in solitude. *Rank*, in the marching sense, came from the same root — what was originally an informal circle of warriors has become a straight line. *Ring* and *rink* are relatives.

HARANGUE

harlot

Old French *arlot*, lad, young fellow, knave, vagabond. This word was entirely masculine. Chaucer wrote: "He [Somonour] was a gentil harlot and a kynde A bettre felawe sholde men noght fynde." *Hoyden* meant boor, clownish man; and *bawd* came from *ribald* (ribaud), "a rogue, ruffian, rascall, scoundrel, varlet, filthie fellow." The girls walked off with the honors in these fields in the fifteenth century.

hippopotamus

Greek, river horse. When the unwieldy beast first dawned on Greek eyes in Africa, looking like nothing they'd ever seen in Zeus' heaven or earth, they employed a metaphor to name it, comparing the unknown with the known — it was a horse or *hippo* (their largest animal) and it lived in a river or *potamus*. *White elephant*, a burdensome possession, is said to get its meaning from a playful custom of Siamese kings, who used to give one of the sacred white elephants to a courtier, who would then quite literally be eaten out of house and home.

WHITE ELEPHANT:
See Hippopotamus

hob-nob

Old English *hæbbe*, have; and *næbbe*, have not. This present term for intimate gossip originally meant have or have not. Shakespeare used it as a synonym for give and take. Later the word was used by two cronies drinking to each other. We think it ought to be revived — lift your glass and say " Hob nob! " Take it or leave it.

hors d'œuvres

French, outside the works. The regular dinner plus. Addison used the expression to mean out of the ordinary course of things, but not in reference to food. He wasn't thinking of coiled anchovies nor of stuffed eggs. The *hors* part comes from the Latin *foris*, outdoors; *œuvres* from *operare*, to work.

humor

Latin (h)*umorem*, fluid, moisture. Galen thought that
there were four chief fluids, the cardinal humours, of
the body — the sanguine humour, blood; phlegm; yel-
low bile or choler; and black bile, melancholy. Thus
we have the four dispositions — sanguine (red corpus-
cles make you bloody hopeful), phlegmatic, choleric,
melancholic. *Temperament* (Latin *tempus*, time) re-
sults when you mix the humours. When Shakespeare
used *humorous* in *Romeo and Juliet* he meant damp.
To speak of " dry humor " seems a bit paradoxical.

ignoramus

Latin phrase, we do not know. A sort of confession of
know-nothingness. Blount's *Law Dictionary* (1691),
says: "Ignoramus (i. e. we are ignorant) is properly
written, on the bill of indictments by the grand enquest
. . . when they mislike their evidence, as defective or
too weak to make good the presentment." There was
a play written in 1615 by Ruggle, intended to expose
the ignorance of the " common lawyers," with Ignoramus as the title-role.

immolate

Latin *immolare*, to sprinkle with sacrificial meal. The Romans, when they got a calf or a bull ready for the slaughter on their altars, prepared the victim. Related words are *mill*, Latin *molere*, and the *meal* itself.

imp

Anglo-Saxon *impa*, shoot, graft. At first *imp* was used as a verb in describing grafting of trees or of inserting feathers into a hawk's wing. The noun acquired the sense of child, offspring, a shoot or graft of human stock. And later, being commonly used in such expressions as "imp of Satan," it reached its present meaning. *Scion* was the French word for shoot for grafting. Two early uses of imp: "Prince Edward, that goodly ympe "; "Art thou . . . that Impe of Glory? "

impecunious

Latin *im-*, not; and *pecu*, cattle. The Romans used cattle as their standard of wealth and their unit of barter long before they had metal coins. Later, the word *pecu* became the name for money. If you were ever so pedantic as to refer to yourself as impecunious rather than broke, you would be saying that you hadn't a sheep to your name nor a cow to bless yourself with. *Pecuniary* is derived from the same root, as is *peculate*, to steal cattle, and *peculiar*, whose original sense was that of cattle belonging exclusively to one man. See *chattel* and *fee*.

indenture

Latin *indentare*, to furnish with teeth. When an agreement was reached between an employer and an apprentice, the articles of *indenture* were torn in half, leaving toothed edges. The genuineness of either half could then be tested — the paper teeth fitted into each other. To *indent* something is to make tooth-marks in it. A *dandelion* is so named from the toothed edge of the leaf, from the French *dent de lion*, tooth of the lion.

INDENTURE

index

Latin, forefinger. Anything that points out or indi-
cates (Latin *dicare*, to make known). Until the sixteenth century an index had nothing to do with a book.

infant

Latin *infans*, unable to speak. To be true to our word,
we ought never to use *infant* of any baby over a year or
thereabouts. Infants' departments in most stores sell
clothes for children up to five — all wrong. And we
are wrong again when we talk of *infantile Leftists*, because they do nothing *but* speak. *Infantry* were so
called because their ranks were made up of youths, able
to walk (and not expected to speak unless spoken to).

ink

Latin *encaustum*, the purple-red ink used by Roman emperors for their official signatures; Greek, burnt in. From the same root as *encaustic*, a burning-in process used in enameling, etc.; and as *caustic*, referring to acid or to speech which burns.

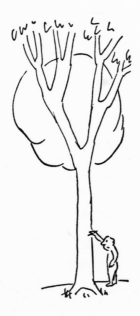

inkling

Middle English *incle*, recorded once only, to whisper. Now used only in phrases such as: " I haven't an inkling," meaning " I haven't even a hint as to the idea," this handy word once served as a verb: " She inkled what it was " — she hinted or whispered. We'd like to see it revived.

INKLING

innuendo

Latin *in*, towards; and *nuere*, to nod. A very subtle way of hinting. Blount's *Glossary* (1674) says: "*Innuendo* is a law term, most used in declarations and other pleadings; and the office of this word is only to declare and ascertain the person or thing which was named uncertain before; that is to say, he (innuendo, the plaintiff) is a thief." The word evidently was synonymous with "to wit," "that is to say." We know a great many lawyers, but they aren't content with nodding.

insult

Latin *in*, upon; and *salīre*, to leap. We do our jumping on people figuratively and orally nowadays, but it sometimes hurts just as much. If we used words accurately, we might say of a football play: "The tackle insulted the player carrying the ball." A related word is *salacious*. When the Romans lusted, they didn't just leer — they leaped.

INSULT

intoxicate

Greek, bow and arrows. From arrows to making drunk is a fairly long trek, which happened this way: we have a Greek word for arrow; from that, a word for poison in which arrows were dipped; from this came the Latin *toxicum*, poison in general; and finally English *intoxicate* — to put poison into someone in the form of liquor. A statement open to argument. In the medical *autointoxication* we have kept the original meaning, as in *toxic* and *antitoxin* (against poison).

iota

Greek letter *i*, the smallest in the alphabet. We always thought of an iota, in phrases such as " It makes not an iota of difference," as being something like a split atom, infinitesimal. We were exaggerating — it could make a tremendous difference, at least in words. A synonym for egotist: *iotacist*. Hint to columnists. *Jot* in such phrases as " It doesn't matter a jot " is merely *iota* Anglicized.

Jack

Hebrew *Johanan*, gift of God; English *John*, of which Jack is a pet name. The word *jack*, spelled without a capital, is one of the most used monosyllables in English. We call almost anybody or anything a jack, for no reason at all. Here's a partial list: a fellow, a lad of the working-classes — " Hey, Jack! "; a sailor; an odd-job man; steeple-jack; the knave in a deck of cards; a machine for turning the spit in roasting; a winch; a boot-jack; a device for hoisting a car; an engine; a part of some musical instruments; a farthing; a quarter of a pint; male birds; male ass; pike; a flag; and money. Our gifts of God are infinite.

January

Latin *Janus*, the ancient Latin deity who guarded doors and entrances. Naturally he looked after the doorway to the New Year, too. Janus had two faces — one looking forward, one back. That useful but humble man the *janitor* derives his title from the same root, *janua*, door. Janus' temple was closed only in times of peace, which were not frequent.

J A N U A R Y

jeans

That all-ages, all-sexes uniform of America, bluejeans, is a sailor's corruption of *Genoa*—the sturdy cerulean cotton cloth having been imported from Italy originally. When we call the material *denim* we are saying cloth *de Nîmes*, from the French city. It was originally *serge de Nîmes*, wool, not cotton overalls stuff. The *London Gazette*, 1703: "A pair of flower'd Serge de Nim Breeches." Too elegant for small-boat sailing by far. *Duffel* is a town of Brabant, near Antwerp, where a coarse woolen cloth was woven—hence duffel bags and duffel coats. *Dungarees* is from the Hindu word *dungri*, an Indian calico, mentioned as early as 1613 in a purchasing list.

journal

Latin *diurnalis*, daily; *dies*, day; through the French where the *d* became a *j*. A weekly journal is an anomaly. *Journalism* came into use in 1833. Originally, a *journey* referred only to the travels or events or work of one day; and a *journeyman* was one who worked by the day. In *Measure for Measure* we have: " His journal greeting " — a synonym for daily.

Kaiser

Latin *Cæsar*, name of Gaius Julius Cæsar. This is the earliest Latin loan-word found in Teutonic. Being impressed by Cæsar's early dictator exploits, the Teutons and the Slavs adopted his name as a generic term for ruler. In the Slavic languages it became *czar* or *tsar*. There is no present tense for this word — it's purely historical. *Emperor* comes similarly from *Imperator* (Latin, commander), a title conferred on Cæsar.

lady

Anglo-Saxon *hlæfdige*, loaf or bread kneader. How times have changed! Your lady of today wouldn't know what to do with a trough of dough if she met one. Yet your Early English lady had to work for her title. If she wanted to be head of her household, she had to feed it. The *lord* was the Anglo-Saxon *hlæf-weard* or loaf-keeper; and the servant a *hlæfæta*, or loaf-eater. Lords and ladies had responsibilities. Hey nonny nonny for the good old days, when lords and ladies baked and employees ate.

lavish

Old French *lavasse*, a deluge of rain; Latin *lavare*, to wash. Originally used as a noun, a synonym for profusion, as in Caxton: "Ther was no lavas in their speche." From the same root: *lava*, meaning originally "a streame or gutter sodainly caused by rain" (to call the molten Vesuvial streams *lava* is to use the word figuratively); *lavatory*, a place for washing; *lavender*, because the plant was used to perfume the bath and to scent clean linens.

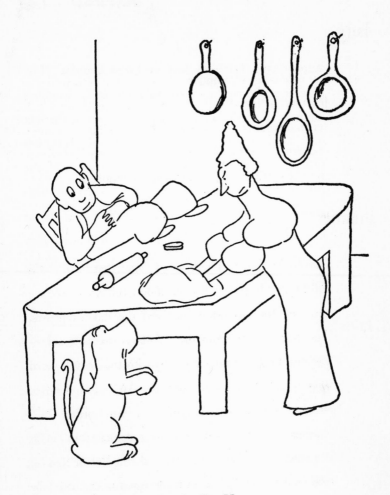

L A D Y

libel

Latin *libellus*, diminutive of *liber*, book. Originally a harmless little book, the word came to mean any brief written legal form, then a leaflet defaming a person's character (1776), and now any defamatory written statement. Quite a change for so innocent a word.

lunatic

Latin *luna*, moon. There was a belief that *lunacy* was caused by sleeping with the moon full on your face and that the condition followed the moon's phases. The *lunatic* was moonstruck. *Loony*, the slang abbreviation, has got itself associated with the Scotch word *loon* which meant lout, from the Anglo-Saxon *lutan*, to bend low, the posture of an inferior order. J. T. says many people think that *loony* comes from "crazy as a loon," because of the maniacal laughter of that big bird as it sits on its tail in the water for take-off. The name of this aquatic creature has nothing to do with the moon. It is an alteration of *loom*, dialect of the Shetland Islands.

L U N A T I C

lust

Anglo-Saxon *lust*, pleasure, delight, enjoyment. A thoroughly innocent word, corrupted through the church. The Latin *concupiscentia carnis* (I John ii, 16) was translated as *lusts of the flesh*, since when *lust* has meant something a little more desirous than plain pleasure to most people. *Lusty* has gone in meaning from joyful, to gaily dressed, to full of sinful desire, to vigorous.

lyceum

Greek, the garden where Aristotle taught at Athens, next to the temple of Apollo, one of whose names was Lyceios, the wolf-slayer. This word has traveled a long way to attach itself to little American groups of serious thinkers and the lecture-courses they arrange. The *Academy* was the grove near Athens where Plato taught, the first *athenæum* was the temple of Athene (Minerva), and the *Stoa* the porch where Zeno lectured — whence our word *stoic*. Not Greek to us at all, but English.

L Y C E U M

macadamize

English. Road-making according to the system of John Landon McAdam (1756–1836). The rubber coat that keeps you dry (maybe) on a rainy day was named for the patenter, Charles *Macintosh*, who died in 1843. Those obsolete carriages called *victorias* were named for Queen V. *Phaeton*, now a type of car, was the foolhardy young son of Apollo who drove his father's chariot across the sky to disaster.

manavilins

This is a handy word I've met only on Nantucket Island, where it is used collectively to describe all the left-over food at the end of summer, a sort of *lagniappe* for the caretaker who closes your house. The origin is obscure, but in Smyth's *Sailor's Word Book*, 1867, *to manarvel* was to pilfer small stores, and an early slang dictionary defines *manavilins* or *menavelings* as broken victuals; odd money after the daily accounts are made up at a railway ticket office—usually divided among the clerks; or small matters, odds and ends generally.

PHAETON:

See Macadamize

maroon

Spanish *cimarron*, wild, untamed. From this word the French evolved *marron*, meaning a fugitive slave in their West Indian colonies. Hence the verb *to maroon* came to mean send astray, put ashore on desert islands. It was so used by Alexander Selkirk, noted marooned sailor serving under Dampier. The word in 1777 or thereabouts was used in the South to mean to camp out for several days on a pleasure party. Odd ideas those Southerners had. Edna Ferber used *Cimarron* as the title of a grand book. The color *maroon* comes from a different source: French *marron*, chestnut.

melancholy

Greek, black bile. The medieval physiologists thought all temperament was produced by *humors* or moistures. A black one made you gloomy or melancholic. A blood-colored one made you cheerful or *sanguine* (Latin *sanguis*, blood). See *humor*.

MAROON

meticulous

Latin *meticulosus*, *metus*, fear. A meticulously, or
fearfully, misused word. To speak of an author's style
as *meticulous* has no meaning at all. Of what is he
afraid? Of course fear breeds timidity, but people who
use *meticulous* as a synonym for careful do not mean
to imply carefulness as a result of timidity. This word
is almost as misused as *demean*, which means how you
behave, your demeanor, and has no connection with
mean in the sense of low or base.

mistletoe

Old German *mist*, dung (perhaps); and Anglo-Saxon
tān, twig. A popular belief, dating to the third century
at least, that the mistletoe plant grew from bird-drop-
pings. If that doesn't ruin romance and kissing next
Christmas, nothing will. *Missel-thrush*, a bird which
feeds on mistletoe berries. Holland, translating Pliny's
Natural History in 1634, wrote: " it [mistletoe] comes
only by the newting of birds — which feed thereupon,
and let it passe through their body."

M I S T L E T O E

mob

Latin *mobile vulgus*, movable, fickle crowd. A short-ened slang word dating from the time of Charles II in England. A writer of the period reports: " I may note that the rabble first changed their title, and were called the ' mob ' in the assemblies of this [The Green Room] Club." The greenroom, a room provided in theaters for actors when not on stage, probably was so-called from some particular London playhouse where the room was decorated in green. The term appears as early as 1701 in Cibber's *Love Makes Man:* "I do know London pretty well, and the Side-box, Sir, and behind the scenes; ay, and the Green-Room, and all the Girls and Women-Actresses there." From the first half of the same root: *automobile* (self-moving), *locomotive* (place moving), *mobilize*.

money

Latin, *Juno Moneta*, the admonishing goddess to whose Roman temple the mint was attached. The first money ever coined in a mint was made here, and called *moneta* in honor of the goddess. *Mint* itself is an Anglo-Saxon evolution from the Latin word. Philosophers to the contrary, *money* is akin to *mind*, both having come ultimately from the Sanskrit *man*, to think, remember. From the same root: *mental, mentor, monitor, mania*.

months

Anglo-Saxon *mōna*, moon. *January* (see). *February*, Latin *februa*, feast of cleansing. *March*, Mars' month. (He has a day, too. See *days*). *April*, from Latin *aprire*, to open — plants coming up and leaves coming out. *May*, the goddess Maia. *June*, from the influential Roman family of Junius. *July*, an honor to Gaius Julius Cæsar. Before Cæsar's day this month was Quintilus, the fifth. *August* is for Augustus Cæsar. The rest of the months are numbered like Fifth Avenue — just seventh, eighth, ninth, tenth.

mountebank

Italian *montambanco*, mount on bench. Your original mountebank got up on a bench or platform at a fair to sell his fake wares or to do juggling tricks. The surname of a noted Massachusetts family, Saltonstall, meant the same originally — Old French *salte-en-estal*, jump on bench. The first name of one Saltonstall — Leverett — means hare. An active fellow.

MOUNTEBANK

muscle

Latin *musculus*, diminutive of mouse. Early anato-
mists fancied that certain muscles looked like mice in
shape. Which ones we don't know, but perhaps " are
we mice or are we men? " contains no dilemma after
all, if muscles *are* mice. A muscular fellow is a little
mousy. That blue Riviera delicacy, the *mussel* you eat,
comes from mouse, too — at least in name.

nainsook

Urdu *nain*, eye; and *sukh*, pleasure. A pleasant name
for a fabric. Many other cloths took their names from
the place where they were first made: *madras*, of which
your father's nightshirts were made, from Madras, India; *cambric* from Cambray, Flanders; *calico* from Cal-
cutta; *cashmere* from the Vale of Kashmir; *damask*
from Damascus; nankeen from Nankin, China; *gauze*
from Palestinian Gaza.

namby-pamby

English literary slang, a corruption of Ambrose. Ambrose Philips, who died in 1749, was a sentimental poet whose style was ridiculed by Carey and Pope. Pope coined Namby-Pamby to use in the *Dunciad* in place of Philips' name.

names

Algernon, Old French, meaning with whiskers. *Cecil*, Latin, dim-sighted. *David*, Hebrew, beloved. *Edward*, Anglo-Saxon, protector of property. *Elliot*, Gaelic, fancy's flight. *Eugene*, Greek, *well-born* (*eugenics*). *Hilary*, Latin, cheerful, merry (*hilarious*). *Ignatz*, Greek, ardent, fiery (*ignite*). *Isaac*, Hebrew, laughter. *John*, Hebrew, gift of God. *Julius*, Latin, soft-haired. *Leopold*, Old High German, lion of the people. *Milton*, Greek, red. *Percival*, Latin, very courteous. *Philip*, Greek, lover of horses. *Quentin*, Latin, the fifth. *Roger*, Old High German, famous with the spear. *Thomas*, Aramaic, twin. Most feminine names are counterparts of masculine ones — Joan from John and so on.

naughty

Late Middle English *nawiht*, no whit, nothing, nought.
Nowadays a nursery word, applied only to children
(or stories). Naughty originally meant having or pos-
sessing *naught*, poor, needy. An early Biblical translation has, in Jeremiah: "The other basket had very
naughty figs." We suppose naughty here refers more
to the figs' rottenness than to their moral state. *Aught*
was the Anglo-Saxon *ā*, ever, and *wiht* (*whit*), thing,
creature. *Naught* or *nought* merely negatived *aught*.

nefarious

Latin *nefas*, wrong, from *ne*, not; and *fas*, right or, literally, divinely spoken. When the gods proclaimed,
everything was O.K. When they didn't, things were
nefarious. *Fame*, *fable*, and *fate* all come from this *fas*,
fari, to speak right. *Fame* merely means of common
report, what people are saying, good or ill.

neighbor

Anglo-Saxon *nēah-gebūr*, literally nigh boor. *Nigh* meant and still means near, next; but *boor* meant husbandman, farmer. It was the city slicker's idea that a country fellow's manners were bad that gives us our use of *boorish*. *The Bowery* (a word from the same root) in New York (then New Amsterdam) was a pleasant green farmy place. Alas! *Neighborhood* used to mean, not a locality, but friendly conduct.

nice

Middle English *nice*, foolish, simple, ignorant. In *Piers Plowman* the word is so used: " For he was nyce, and ne couthe no wisdom " — for he was foolish and knew no wisdom. In Chaucer: " wise and nothing nice " — wise and not at all simple. The word came to have its present meaning of fastidious, dainty, delicious, perhaps through confusion with *nesh*, which meant delicate. We use this overworked and confused little word even as an adverb in phrases such as " nice and hot," " nice and early." In the original sense, *nice* is related to the Latin *nescius*, ignorant, no science.

nickname

Anglo-Saxon *eac*, to augment, to add to; and *nama*, name. Originally, *an eke-name*, the word became *neke-name*, borrowing the *n* from the *an*, then finally nickname. Something added to your regular name.

nicotine

French proper name, *Nicot*. Jacques Nicot, French ambassador at Lisbon, sent some tobacco plants to Catherine de' Medici in or about 1560. The drug was named for him. Many names of things are derived from their inventors or from someone associated with their use: four electrical terms — *Watt* (James Watt, inventor of the steam engine), *ampere*, *ohm*, *volt*; *fuchsia* from a German botanist Fuchs; *sadist* from the Count de Sade; the *saxophone* from its inventor, Adolphe Sax; and *venereal* disease for Venus, goddess of love (profane).

NICOTINE

nincompoop

Latin *non compos mentis*, not in possession of one's mind. The phrase was shortened to *non compos*, then corrupted by British tongues to its present form. A very learned way of calling an acquaintance a simpleton. It was used in *The Guardian* in 1713: "An old niny-hammer, a dotard, a nincompoop." *Ninny*, associated with nincompoop in meaning, was a pet name for the proper name Innocent; much as the word for an idiot, *cretin*, came from a Swiss dialect form of *Christian*.

obbligato

Italian, obliged. That is, an indispensable accompaniment. Most of our musical terms are borrowed straight from Italian: *piano*, short for *pianoforte*, which means soft-strong, or from treble to bass. *Basso* is Italian for low. Non-musical words related to obbligato: *oblige, ally, ligament, ligature, lien, liability, league.* See *assets.*

OBBLIGATO

O.K.

U.S. slang in use since about 1790. There are several stories as to the derivation of this ineluctable expression — one, that it was an abbreviation for the facetious " orl korrect "; another, that it was adapted from the Choctaw Indian word *okeh* meaning " It is so and in no other way "; and a third, that the finest rum and molasses brought from Aux Cayes in Haiti was marked OK — phonetic shorthand for the port of shipment.

onion

Latin *unus*, one; *ūniōnem*, unity, union. An onion has many layers of skin united into one globe. Since the union of A.F. of L. and C.I.O., they are more *onion* than ever — in other words, united. An olfactory symbol of the United States: an onion rampant with its multifold layers wrapped as one. Your student of words knows his onions.

opportune

Latin *op-*, *ob-*, toward; and *Portumus*, protecting god
of harbors, from *portus*, harbor. Whatever is opportune — fit, suitable, appropriate, convenient — is pleas-
ing to the god who looks after happy landings. In
other words, you can arrive at the opportune: it is ac-
cessible. The reverse is *importunate* — *im-* being the
Latin negative. *Opportunist* was coined in France in
1876 by Rochefort in reference to Gambetta and his
followers.

orient

Latin *oriri*, to rise. The Orient is where the sun rises,
in the east — a purely occidental-eye-view. *Occident*
comes from the Latin *ob-* or *oc-* and *cadere*, to fall —
where the sun sets, the west. *Orientation* is adapted
from the French *s'orienter*, to take one's bearings, literally to turn oneself to the east. *Accident* comes from
the same root as *occident* — what befalls. Since *ori-
ental* merely means eastern, *we* are orientals to the Japanese, who look eastward to see us.

pandemonium

Greek *pan*, all; and *dæmonium*, evil spirit. Coined by Milton to describe the capital of Hell, abode of all the demons. "Pandæmonium, the high Capital Of Satan and his Peers." *Demonifuge* is a charm against demons, in case you want to know. From the Latin *fuga*, flight, as in the musical term, *fugue*.

panic

Greek *Pan*, god of shepherds, flocks, country music. He also caused, in his prankish way, noises which produced groundless terror in mortal listeners. *Panic*, at first used as an adjective married to terror — panic terror — became a synonym for fear, terror. Later *Pan* became the impersonation of all nature in people's minds — a confusion with the Greek combining form *pan-*, meaning all.

PANDEMONIUM

pansy

French *pensée*, thoughtful; Latin *pensare*, to weigh, ponder. Can't you see the pansy's velvet thoughtful little face pondering? *Tulip* is another image-word. It comes from the Persian *dulband*, turban, which an open tulip undoubtedly resembles in shape and color and satin texture. *Nasturtium* is the Latin for nose-twist, because of its pungency. Pliny wrote: " nomen accepit a narium tormento " — a name received from tormenting of the nose.

paraphernalia

Greek, beyond, beside; and *dowry*, that which is brought by a wife. Blackstone, in his *Commentaries*, says: " In one particular instance the wife may acquire a property in some of her husband's goods; which shall remain to her after his death, and not go to his execu-tors. These are called her *paraphernalia*, which is a term borrowed from the civil law." So, gentlemen, when you ask your wife if she has packed all her *paraphernalia* for the trip, be careful. You are admit-ting those things belong to her.

pardon

Latin *per*, thoroughly; and *donare*, to give. The Old French form was *perdun* — a comforting pronunciation to Arthur Kober's Bronx characters. Remember, when you grant a pardon to someone — give it thoroughly.

parliament

French *parlement*, a speaking. If you have ever sat in the Visitors' Gallery at Westminster, you know that's what they do. Here, here, here, here! Hear, hear, hear, hear! Havelok in 1006, before the Normans got to England, spoke in Middle English of a *parlement*. *Parley* comes from the same root, and *parlor*, a place in which to talk — so please move the T.V. set into the rumpus-room and let us talk. *Rumpus* is an eighteenth-century fanciful coinage meaning riot, disturbance, uproar. Mademoiselle from Armentières, *parlez-vous?* A kind of gingerbread was called *parliament* in 1812. We wonder why. See *senate*.

penthouse

Latin *appendicium*, appendage. What so proudly we hail as the tops of all modern city dwellings is thus akin to that functionless organ doctors are eternally carving out of us. The original word was *pentis*, a lean-to with a one-slope roof. Early associated with French *pente*, slope, popular etymology invented *penthouse*. Scott wrote: "There . . . lurked under the penthouse of his eye that sly epicurean twinkle." Ever lurk under any penthouses? We advise against it. You might get eavesdroppings in your hair.

pioneer

Old French *peon*, a foot-soldier. The boys who went ahead of the army to clear away forests and dig trenches. We see the fitness of this metaphor in describing those pioneers of the United States who vanguarded the westward movement. The name of the humble little piece in chess called a *pawn* comes from the same root, and certainly he pioneers before the King, the Queen, the Knight, and the rest of the aristocracy.

PIONEER

plunder

Middle German *plunder*, bedclothes, household stuff. By transference, this domestic and intimate word came to mean the stealing of such articles, and later any pillaging of goods. A chronicle of 1647 says: " Many Townes and Villages he [Prince Rupert] plundered, which is to say robb'd, for at that time first was the word plunder used in England, being borne in Germany."

posh

When the British say something is *posh*—and the word is heard here more and more often—they mean it is fashionable, elegant, grand. There is a folk-etymology for it which I like. When top brass travelled to India in the viceregal old days, by steamer, the preferred cabins were, because of the sun's heat, on the port side out, starboard home—hence *posh*, from the initials P, O, S, H.

precocious

Latin *pre-*, before; and *coquere*, to cook. The precocious child is like a steak broiled too soon for dinner. The term was first applied to plants which ripened early. Sir Thomas Browne in the seventeenth century talked of "precocious Figgs." *Dementia præcox* as a psychological term means out of your mind before you're really off the fire.

preposterous

Latin *pre-*, before; and *posterus*, coming after. A preposterous situation is one in which that which should
be first comes last. Another case of cart-before-the-
horse, hindside before, topsy-turvy.

proletariat

Latin *proles*, offspring. The Latin word *proletarius*
meant a citizen of the lowest class, scorned politically
and economically, but regarded as useful as being a
parent. Evidently neither the term nor the idea was invented by Karl Marx. Butler, in *Hudibras*, spoke of
" Low proletarian tything men." Another earlier English source says: " Such men were y-cloped proletarii,
that is geteris of children." The political currency of
the word in such phrases as *dictatorship of the prole-
tariat* was minted by nineteenth-century French econ-
omists. *Prolific* means, literally, making offspring.
Now generally used of authors. The Greeks said *hoi
polloi* — referring to the masses, not to authors.

PREPOSTEROUS

propaganda

Latin *propago*, a slip or shoot for transplanting. This word, considered menacing in the democracies of to-day, was at first a botanist's term for multiplying plants by taking slips. Soon it came to mean the spreading or *propagation* of ideas by transplanting brain-shoots. True education leads out the abilities inside the student, develops him. A *student* is an eager person — from the Latin *studere*, to be zealous. *Study* is from *studium*, eager attention. The original sense of zealousness is kept in "studied insult." Other words from the root *educare*, to lead out: *duke, aqueduct, conduct, viaduct, induce, reduce, Il Duce*. Il Duce reminds us that there is nothing toxic in the word *propaganda* itself; its venom evolved from its use by Fascist and Communist against democracy. *Propaganda* was first used in the title *Congregatio de Propaganda Fide*, a committee of cardinals of the Roman Catholic Church founded in 1622 to supervise foreign missions.

protocol

Greek, the first leaf of a volume, a fly-leaf glued to the binding and containing an account of the manuscript. When *protocol* is used in its modern diplomatic sense of which dignitary's wife shall march in to dinner first, it seems to us the glue is very sticky for employment in a democracy.

prude

French *preux*, Latin *prodesse*, to be of value. This word, now one of the most insulting you can be called, once meant the same as *proud*, which stems from the same Latin root, and as *prowess*. To be a prude was to be, in old France, valiant, courageous, full of prowess, notable. A *prude femme* was a discreet, an excellent woman. The gallant has become the prig. *Prig* meant in seventeenth-century slang a petty thief. It has been guessed that its present sense comes from a different source — a foreshortening of " precisionist," or it may be from " to prick," in the obsolete sense of dressing up.

quack

Dutch *kwakzalver*, one who sells his salves by his pat-
ter or quacking. Hence, a phony doctor. *Quack* itself
is an imitative word — what the duck says. *Quack* in
the sense of fake doctor is short for *quacksalver*.
Quack in the sense of Donald Duck's speech is short
for a string of abuse.

quaint

Old French *cointe*, Latin *cognitum*, known. Here is a
word that has changed unrecognizably. Originally in
English it meant clever, ingenious, neat, fine, spruce,
brisk, dainty, tricked up. In Latin it was similar to our
acquaint, to make known. Things which were ingeniously or cunningly designed and made were quaint.
In later machine-age days it was the old-fashioned
and hand-made that looked ingenious and charming —
hence our use of quaint as applied to Nantucket houses
or to old-fashioned manners. See *nice*.

QUACK

quarantine

Latin *quaranta*, forty. The period of isolation for contagious diseases used to be forty days, no matter what you had. In law, quarantine denoted the forty days' grace in which a widow had the right to remain in the chief mansion-house of her dead husband. From an antique English author: " If she marry within the forty days she loseth her quarentine."

radical

Latin *radix*, root. Originally meaning pertaining to roots of trees or plants, then a mathematical formula, next used to designate a primitive or basic word, *radical* now means to most people a Red, a Leftist. This extremist sense of *radical* came about, of course, because of the radical's desire to tear things up by the roots. A radical change is a change from the roots up. The first use in a political sense dates from the early eighteenth century, in " radical reform." *Radish* (a root itself) is from the same stem. It's red, too.

RADICAL

℞

Latin *recipe*, take. This mysterious notation, used by doctors and pharmacists as a bit of magic to make that prescription look more effective, means nothing more nor less occult than — take it. It's the same imperative you find in any cook-book — a *recipe*. Take two eggs. Separate them. *Receipt* and *receive* are the same, literally " again take." *Conceit* (take together) and *deceit* (take down) are relatives.

regalia

Latin *rex*, king, *regalis*, regalia, royal. Strictly speaking, *regalia* are royal powers, rights and privileges, and not those decorations, plumes, and medals worn by Knights of Columbus, Shriners, and other brotherhoods. Superior Cuban cigars are called *regalia* because they were formerly manufactured by special privilege (and tax) of the Spanish King.

reject

Latin *re-*, back; and *jacere*, throw. A brutal gesturing word. When you reject a suitor, you throw him back on his heels. When an editor rejects a manuscript, he throws it back in your trash-basket. *Inject* is to throw in, *project* is to throw forth, and *adjective* is a descriptive word you throw *at* a noun.

remorse

Latin *remordeo*, to bite again. In other words, when you're in anguish for something you have done, or not done, or said, conscience bites man. The English of Chaucer's day called it the *ayenbite of inwit* — the again bite of inner knowledge. Moderns prefer the compact Latin word. *Mordant* is from the same root.

rigmarole

Sixteenth-century England, *ragman-roll*, a list, a cata-
logue. The original Ragman's Roll was a record of
homage made to Edward I by the Scottish King and
nobles in 1296. There was a medieval game of *ragman*,
dealing with incoherent lists of words. *Ragman* even
earlier seems to have been *rageman*, a justice appointed
by Edward I to hear complaints.

rival

Latin *rivus*, stream; *rivalis*, one living on the opposite
bank of a stream from another. Since rivers were natural boundaries in early days, and men none too neigh-
borly, the figurative meaning is easy to understand.
Rivals want the same thing — same fish in the stream,
same job, same girl. See *arrive.*

RIVAL

Rotten Row

French *route du roi*, road of the king. This elegant
pony-path in England's Hyde Park, seemingly so inele-
gantly named, shows how words change when borrowed by another land.

roué

French *rouer*, to break on the wheel. The Duke of
Orléans, profligate Regent of France during the mi-
nority of Louis XV, collected a fine group of rapscal-
lion companions about him and affectionately called
them his *roués* — because there wasn't one who didn't
deserve to be broken on the wheel, the current punish-
ment for criminals. From the same root (ultimately,
Latin *rota*, wheel): *Rotary* Club, *rotation, roulette,
rotogravure*.

ruminate

Latin *rumen*, throat, *ruminari*, to chew the cud. When you ruminate on your problems, you are like a thoughtful cow chewing her cud.

salary

Latin, *salarium*. Originally, salt-money, or money given to the soldiers for salt. If you have no job and feel that life without a salary is flavorless, you aren't far from the word's derivation. My learned sources make no mention of " salt it away," but I like to think there's a relationship. In India British officers get an extra allowance called *batta*, from *bhatta*, rice.

sandwich

Named after John Montagu, Fourth Earl of Sandwich (1718–92), who once spent twenty-four hours at the gaming-table without sitting down to a regular meal — and they *were* regular in the eighteenth century. The legend goes that he ordered his man to bring him bread and roast-beef which he united to make the world happier and Reubens' Restaurant an institution. The *sandwich-man*, a slice of humanity between two advertising boards, was first seen in 1864. The Earl of Sandwich got his title from the Anglo-Saxon Sandwic, or sand village, in Kent.

sarcasm

Greek; literally, to tear flesh like dogs; hence, to bite the lips in rage, to sneer. Being sarcastic is a top-lofty and conceited activity at best. Next time you're tempted, think of yourself as gnawing meat, dog-like. Hint for making friends and winning people. *Mordant* also means to bite, from the Latin *mordere*, to bite. See *remorse*.

SANDWICH

satellite

Latin *satellitem*, attendant or guard. A very early word now much in use in two modern senses: first, for the countries behind the Iron Curtain, such as Hungary and Czechoslovakia, which have lost their independent identities and are now mere guards or attendants on Soviet Russia; second, for the Sputniks and Explorers we and Russia are rocketing into outer space to orbit around Earth. *Satellites* was first applied by Kepler in 1611 to the secondary planets revolving around Jupiter, recently discovered by Galileo. *Satellite* as applied to people has a reproachful connotation, implying subservience, sometimes unscrupulous.

scaramouch

Italian *scaramuccia*, skirmish. This stock character in Italian farce, a boastful poltroon, always enters into skirmishes with Harlequin, hence his name. We would like to see the use of this mouth-filling word extended. For example: " The Yale team entered into a bloody scaramouch with Harvard." *Scrimmage* comes from the same root.

school

Greek, leisure. Not many children of school age will admit that they spend their days in leisure; though many of us in looking backward see the truth in this derivation — leisure to learn, leisure to develop. *Seminary* comes from the Latin *seminarium*, seed-bed, a place where little scholars may be cultivated. Other words from the same root: *semen; disseminate*, to scatter seed.

schooner

New England *scoon* or *scun*, to skim along over the water. There is a Scandinavian verb *scon*, send over the water. Schooners were first built at Gloucester, Massachusetts, around 1715. *Sloop* is from the Dutch *sloep*, cognate with *to slip*. *Shallop* was an early synonym for sloop. *Clipper ship* came from the Dutch *klepper*, a swift-trotting horse. Hence, figuratively, a fast sailing ship. The *clip* was the sound of the hoof-beat. *Dinghy* was Hindu for dug-out.

senate

Latin *senex*, old; *senatus*, council of old men. A slander
on those legislative boys in Washington equal to calling
the members of the Supreme Court the " nine old
men." In Rome the senate was the council of the elders.
Congress comes from the Latin *congressus*, a coming
or walking together.

SENATE

serendipity

This is a delicious word, newly in style, but coined in 1754 by Horace Walpole. It has nothing to do with *serenity* (Latin *serenus*, clear, fair, calm) but was formed by adding a suffix to *Serendip*, a former name for Ceylon. Walpole writes in a letter that he had formed it upon the title of the fairy-tale "The Three Princes of Serendip," the heroes of which "were always making discoveries by accidents and sagacity, of things they were not in quest of." You go out to a dinner party and meet the man you'll eventually marry. That's *serendipity*.

sherry

Spanish *vino de Xeres*, wine from Xeres, now Jerez. Other articles named for their place of origin: *currants* from Corinth; *port* from Oporto; *meander*, the name of a wandering stream of Phrygia; *muslin*, Italian *mussolina*, from Mosul on the Tigris; *morocco* and *cordovan* leathers from Spain; *pistol* from Pistoja in Spain, and *spaniel*, Spanish dog; *milliner* from Milan; and *italics* from Italy, a type introduced by Aldus Manutius of the famous Aldine Press in Venice in 1501.

shibboleth

Hebrew, meaning sometimes an ear of corn, sometimes a rustling river. A word picked by the Hebrews as a test-word, a pass-word, because the Ephraimites, who weren't allowed to play, couldn't pronounce *sh*. See Judges xii, 6, if you want the whole story. The Italians in the Sicilian massacre of the French in 1282 used *cicera* (chick-peas) as a similar test-word. Modern equivalent: being asked by a small-town cop who suspects you of driving while drunk to say "truly rural" or "Sister Susie sewing shirts for soldiers" or "she sells seashells."

significant

Latin *signum*, mark, token, sign; and *facio*, to make. Gestures were used by mankind before language, so it is fitting that our word for important, full of meaning, should be, literally, making signs. To *signify* your intention is to give a token. When you place your *signature* at the bottom of a letter, you make your mark. To *design* is to mark out; *insignia* are tokens, not necessarily of office.

SIGNIFICANT

silly

Anglo-Saxon *gesælig*, happy, prosperous, fortunate. This word seems to have slipped a little with the centuries. Or do we consider those too silly to know what's going on in the world the fortunate? The Dutch *zalig* means blessed, as does the German *selig*. In England, a cricket term for a spot dangerously near the wicket is *silly*. The silly season was *Punch's* way of referring to the no-news months, August and September. Unhappily no longer true after 1938. In 1939 in August, Hitler declared war.

siren

Greek fancy ladies, part woman, part bird, who lured sailors to shipwreck through their enchanting singing. How do we get from mythology to that blood-curdling shriek which heralds a racing fire-engine? Surely it doesn't enchant us, splitting quiet night streets with dread; but in a way it draws us and lures us to follow it, just as the sirens did Ulysses and his mariners.

skyscraper

Not invented by those picturesque and salty Americans
to describe the Flatiron Building. *Skyscraper* was a
term used by nautical gents as early as 1794 to describe
a triangular sky-sail. *Sky* itself is the Old Norse word
for cloud. In Norway you can't have a cloudless sky,
apparently. *Sky-pilot,* meaning a minister, was a sailors' word, too. Long before airplanes, we find this
word in use: 1888, Churchward in *Blackbirding* — "A
dock missionary (we called him sky-pilot)"; and in
Spectator, 30 December 1893 — "A sky-pilot, in sailor's
parlance, is a clergyman generally, and specially a
clergyman who has a spiritual charge among seamen."

slave

Medieval Latin *slavus*, *Slav*. The Slavs of Central Europe — Russians, Poles, Czechs, Bulgars — were conquered and reduced to slavery. Their racial name became the word for loss of freedom, though its original Slavonic meaning was glory, according to Gibbon, the historian.

solecism

Greek, speaking incorrectly, like an inhabitant of Soloi in Cilicia. Soloi was colonized by emigrants from Athens, whose pure Attic was soon corrupted. A bit of Hellenic snobbery toward any speech except their own. See *barbarian*. Brahmin Bostonians feel that way about the New York dialect. Our word *laconic* comes from the Athenian contempt for the brevity of Spartan, or Laconian, speech.

spirit

Latin *spiritus*, breathing, breath, air. As near as early theologians could come to naming the part of us which isn't tangible. Medieval scientists believed in three spirits or subtle fluids pervading the individual — animal spirits, so called from the Latin *animale*, having the breath of life. They didn't at all mean high jinks on New Year's Eve, now generally attributed to animal spirits. *Inspire* means literally to breathe into; *expire*, to breathe out; *perspire*, to breathe through.

stallion

Old High German *stal*, a stall, stable, a fixed place or station; Italian *stallone*, a horse kept in a stall for stud purposes and not made to work in the fields. The dictionaries genteelly called a stallion an "entire horse." *Horse* itself is derived from the Latin *cursus*, running, from which we get directly our *courser*. A *courier* is a runner, and *current* events running events. A current in a river runs, and so does an electric current.

subtle

Latin *sub*, under; and *texla*, *tela*, woven stuff, web. A subtle odor or a subtle idea are both fine-spun, tenuous, under a veil. In Chaucer's day the spelling was nearer the pronunciation: *sotel* or *sutel*. *Toil*, in the sense of a net or snare for birds, comes from the same root, the French having changed *tela* to *toile*. *Toilette* was originally a small cloth on a dressing-table; and a *text* that which is woven, a fabrication.

C O U R I E R :
See Stallion

succinct

Latin *suc-* (for *sub*), under, below; and *cingere*, to gird. A succinct remark, short, concise, is like a Roman toga girded up closely about the waist. The French term for pregnant, *enceinte*, means girdled. A *cincture* is a belt.

supercilious

Latin *super*, above; and *cilium*, an eyelid. When you conceitedly express disdain, pride, and haughtiness by raising your eyebrows, you are acting out the word *supercilious* more literally than you think. Fine for charades.

SUPERCILIOUS

tandem

Latin *tandem*, at length. An expression meant to describe time has been taken over jokingly to name a team of horses harnessed at length, one before the other. *Reins* comes from the Latin *retinēre*, to hold back; *harness* from a French word meaning gear, especially armor; *bridle* from Anglo-Saxon *bregdan*, to pull, turn, jerk. *Braid* is from the same root. To *upbraid* someone you pull in the reins sharply.

tattoo

Dutch *tap*, a tap; and *toe*, shut, closed, put to. The drum beat a *taptoe* or *tattoo* when it was time for the innkeeper to close his taps and serve the last round of ale or beer. A tattoo is still a signal for shutting up, for a conclusion, whether of soldiers or of arguments. The other sort of tattoo, the artistic sailor's delight, comes from a Tahitian word, *ta*, meaning a mark.

TATTOO

taxicab

Short for *taximeter-cabriolet*, first seen on the streets of London in 1907. The meaning of the various compounds is: *taxi*, Latin *taxare*, to censure, charge, rate, value; later, to impose a tax; *meter*, Greek for measure; *cabriolet* or *cab*, from the French *capriole*, the capering or leaping of a goat. And so, forewarned, you will no longer expect a bounceless ride. (See *capricious*.)

Tenderloin

U.S. slang name applied around 1895 to the police district embracing most of the Broadway theaters, hotels, and other places of amusement, because a certain police captain, having been transferred to the old Twenty-ninth precinct, declared that, after having eaten chuck steak for so long, he would eat *tenderloin* — the juiciest cut, from the point of view of graft and police blackmail. *Porterhouse* remains a steak, though as a word it started as a house or inn frequented by porters who, back in the early 1800's, evidently knew a good steer when they saw one.

testify

Latin *testis*, witness, also *testicle;* and *facio*, to make. Dating back to Biblical times, a witness swore to the truth, or *testified*, by placing his hand on the source of life and manhood, the testes. The King James version, in a polite euphemism, says that an oath is taken by placing the hand upon the thigh. In law, a *testament* is a written and witnessed will; the Old and New Testaments referred to the witnessed covenant between God and man. *Detest* is from *de*, down or away, plus witness.

thug

Hindu *thag*. One of an association of professional robbers and murderers in India. Their favorite method of terminating a victim was strangling, called *thuggee*. This word *thug* has gone a bit sissy in the United States, we think. Your present-day thug is a ruffian but not usually a strangler.

treacle

Greek, pertaining to wild or venomous beasts. This word may be as slow as molasses, but it has moved far in the course of its history. Among the Greeks and Latins the word came to mean, not the bite of a wild or poisonous beast, but an antidote for the bite. From that, it became any remedy. Remedies were generally sticky and syrupy; so eventually *treacle* meant syrup. Chaucer called Christ the " treacle of every harm." He didn't mean molasses, obviously.

trivial

Latin *tri-*, three; and *via*, way. What you pick up at the crossroads, where three ways meet, is of little worth. You hear or see nothing eclectic on the highway. It's commonplace. Don't estimate as important the gossip you hear there or the girls lounging against the signpost. Modern substitute for the crossroad is Café Society. *Trivial* is a slightly snobbish word; sometimes there is wisdom to be met at the crossroads, we have found in our vagabondage.

TRIVIAL

trophy

Greek, to turn. After the enemy was turned or put to flight, a memorial was set up on the battlefield. Metaphorically, your silver cup won in a golf tournament or in a yacht race is just such a memorial of an enemy (friendly) put to flight. *Tropic* pertains to the *turning* of the sun at the solstice. *Heliotrope* is a flower that turns toward the sun (Greek *helios*, sun).

tycoon

Chinese *ta*, great; and *kiun*, prince. A word we thought *Time Magazine* invented to label economic royalists. It was the title by which the Shogun of Japan was described to foreigners. The Japanese borrowed the word from China, making it *taikun*.

TROPHY

ugly

Old Norse *ugga*, to fear. The original sense is kept in the pugilistic phrase " ugly customer," and in " ugly weather " — ominous clouds, dreaded by mariners. There used to be an adjective *ugsome*, meaning horrible, loathsome. *Pretty* meant to the Anglo-Saxons tricky, wily, crafty. From this it came to mean clever, skillful; then brave, gallant; a pretty fellow in the eighteenth century was a fop, a swell — hence to our present trite pink-and-white meaning.

ultramarine

Latin *ultra*, beyond; and *mare*, sea. Originally this word meant what it said. Standing on the New England coast, Nantucket Island would be *ultramarine*. Immigrants were called ultramarine, because they came from beyond the sea. Originally the reference was not to sea-color at all, but to the foreign origin of lapis lazuli, from which the pigment was obtained. *Lapis lazuli* — the Latin words for stone and blue — are two of the loveliest words in English to say. *Azure* comes from the same root as *lazuli*, both originally Persian.

U G L Y

umbrage

French *ombrage*, a shadow; Latin *umbra*, shade. You take umbrage — our only use of the word — when you are thrown in the shade by someone. There was a term in early French horsemanship, *cheval ombrageux*, a horse quick to take flight at its own shadow, which may have influenced our use of *umbrage*. The first *umbrellas* were to cast a shade, not to keep off the rain. The painter's *umber* comes from Italian *terra d'ombra*, shadow earth, a pigment used for shading. "In high *dudgeon*" comes, circuitously, from the same root.

umpire

Middle English *noumper*, Old French *nomper* (non pair), not equal, not a peer. An umpire is a third, extra man called in when two others disagree. The *n* of the old word was lost just as it was lost from *apron*, originally *naperon*, as in *napery* and *napkin*. *Peer* is from the Latin *par*, equal. *Peerless*, without equal; *compare*, equal with. *Peer* in the sense of British nobility is derived from Charlemagne's twelve peers, all equal knights.

UMBRAGE

untrammelled

Latin *un*, not; *tri*, three; and *macula*, mesh. A *trammel* is a long, narrow fishing net, originally (pre-nylon) with three layers of mesh. So when you are in a high and headlong mood — *untrammelled* — you have cleared the net, you are as free-wheeling as a finny fish or a flying bird. Steele and Swift in the *Tatler* (1709) wrote: "The Gentleman is in the true Trammels of Love." Braided hair used to be called "bound up in trammels."

urbane

Latin *urbs*, city. All people who were city-dwellers were smooth, courteous, urbane, while the man from the country (Latin *rus*) was an awkward *rustic*. In Anglo-Saxon times a *boor* was just a farmer (*gebur*) and to be called a *churl* was no insult at all — a *ceorl* was simply a husband. Sometimes he still is, we admit. Later, a churl came to mean a countryman, peasant: low persons supposed, by the aristocracy, to have no manners.

vague

Latin *vagus*, wandering. From the same root: *vagabond*, one who wanders; *vagary*, originally a devious journey, now a caprice of fortune or of the mind; *vagrant* and *vagrancy*; the *vagus* nerve, the pneumogastric nerve which does a bit of straying around the body.

vanilla

Spanish *vainilla*, diminutive of *vaina*, pod, from Latin *vagina*, sheath or scabbard. *Chocolate* was a Mexican word, *chocolatl*. The drink was introduced into England about 1600. Says Pepys on November 24, 1664: " To a coffee-house, to drink jocolatte, very good."

vaudeville

French *Vau de Vire*, Valley of Vire. The word was applied originally to songs from this valley in Calvados, Normandy, specially those light and popular numbers attributed to Olivier Basselin in the fifteenth century. He lived in the valley.

vegetable

Latin *vegere*, to be healthy. Cooper's Latin dictionary, 1573, defines *vegetus* as " quicke, sound, lusty, fresh, lively." Our modern idea of *vegetate* is just the opposite of the original, but the vitamin boys and Popeye have it right. *Fruit* comes from *fructus*, Latin for enjoyment.

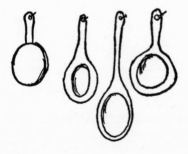

verdict

Anglo-French *veir*, true; and *dit*, says. The twelve
good men and true, and the judge, are bound by etymology always to hand down a truthful judgment. If
this be true, how come so many miscarriages of justice?
Tom Mooney would never have been in jail twenty
years if he had really received a *ver*dict.

V E R D I C T

vernacular

Latin *verna,* bond servant, a home-born slave; *vernaculis,* " that is borne in ons owne house; that taketh beginning in our owne countrey," indigenous, domestic. If you speak in the *vernacular* — and who doesn't? — you speak in what was formerly called the *vulgar* tongue — from Latin *vulgus,* the common people. Another degenerated word. The edition of the Bible known as the *Vulgate* comes from *Editio Vulgata,* literally an edition made public — published — for everyday people.

villain

Old French *vilain,* peasant; Latin *villa,* farm, country house. A *villain* (or *villein*) under the feudal system was not a low and wicked character but merely a serf attached to a manor, a tenant in the villeiny or country estate of some lord. The degeneration of this word came about in much the same way as did that of *churl* and *boor,* both originally just farmers. (See *neighbor* and *urbane.*) Aristocrats thought anyone from the peasant class ill-mannered, rude, and finally *villainous.*

VILLAIN

virtue

Latin *vir*, a man. Originally an instance of masculine conceit — *virtuous* meant full of manly excellence — the feminists of the world have made inroads on virtue till it is almost a womanly quality these days. *Virile* still means manly. A *virago* in Rome was a manlike maiden, a female warrior. In fact she still is. *Virtuoso* was an Italian word coined to describe a virtuous person skilled in the fine arts.

vogue

French *voguer*, to sail forth; Italian *vogare*, to row in a galley or any boat; Old High German *wāc*, wave. And won't this one surprise Condé Nast and the ladies who read *Vogue*. The original sense is " the swaying motion of a ship "; hence the swing, drift, or course of any style, whether mental or fashionable.

weather

Anglo Saxon *weder*, from Sanskrit *va*, to blow. So in an etymological sense, calm weather is really impossible. (For *calm*, see *halcyon*.) Sailors use the *Beaufort Scale* to indicate wind force—from 0 or calm to 12 or hurricane, arranged by Admiral Sir Francis Beaufort (1774-1857) in 1806. *Hurricane*, force 12, "that which no canvas could withstand," as many a luckless sailor knows, comes via Spanish from a Carib Indian word *uracan*, a West Indies cyclone. There is a Mexican god of storm called *Hurakon*. Another theory—folk etymology—derives the name of the storm from the cry of sugar plantation workers when the master wind is coming: "Hurry! Cane!" Get your crop cut while you can. *Gale*, the next force, comes (perhaps) from Danish *gal*, mad, furious. *Storm* comes from an Old Teutonic root, *sturjan*, stir, make a disturbance, which is what wind and waves do. *Tornado:* Latin *tonare*, thunder; or possibly Spanish *tornar*, turn, a revolving storm. *Extonare* means strike by thunder (or its lightning). See *astonish*.

wench

Anglo-Saxon *wencel*, child, boy or girl. Ormulum, in the thirteenth century, uses this word in the account of the birth of the infant Jesus, to indicate a *boy* baby, and certainly with none of our present-day meaning. A *hussy* was just a housewife originally; and *knave* meant boy, with no moral turpitude attached.

whisky

Celtic Irish *uisge beatha, usque baugh*, water of life. Since we have dropped the " of life," our word whisky means water. Well! Other countries serve water of life, too — *aqua vitæ, eau-de-vie, vodka*, which is a diminutive of the Russian word *voda*, water. *Brandy* is short for Dutch *brandewijn*, burnt wine; *gin* for geneva, Latin *juniperus*, whose berries flavor it; and *rum* for rum bullion. *Rum* was a common sixteenth-century synonym for good; perhaps the bullion is from French *bouillon*, any hot drink.

yacht

Dutch *jagt schip*, hunting boat, fast piratical craft. So called because these pleasure-craft — introduced into England from Holland by Charles II — had the sure speed and swiftness of a huntsman. The appearance of these sailboats was a big event in sporting circles. All the diarists of the day wrote it up in their seventeenth-century " Yachting." " I sailed this morning with his Majesty in one of his yachts (or pleasure boats), vessels not known among us till the Dutch East India Company presented that curious piece to the king " — Evelyn, October 1, 1661.

Yankee

U.S. eighteenth century. Probably this nickname was first used of the Dutch inhabitants of New Amsterdam and was a diminutive of *Jan*, John, or a popular way of saying *Jan Kes*, John Cornelius, used by the Dutch as we use John Henry to indicate Everyman. *Yankee notions* were not ideas but small wares made in the Northern states.

index

233

Margaret S. Ernst

was born in 1894 in Natchez, Mississippi. Graduated from Wellesley in 1916, she then went to work on the New Orleans Times-Picayune as reporter, feature writer, and staff poet (poems to order for all occasions). In 1929 she joined the staff of the City and Country School in New York, and there developed her methods of teaching language by means of word study—the basis for her text-book, *Words* (Knopf). Mrs. Ernst is the wife of Morris L. Ernst, the well-known lawyer and author.

James Thurber

was born in Columbus, Ohio, in 1894. After two years with the State Department as a code clerk (1918-1920) he became a reporter for the Columbus Dispatch—and since then has made the world a brighter place with his plays, essays, cartoons, and books. Among his most recent works are *The Years With Ross* (Atlantic-Little, Brown), *The Wonderful O* (Simon and Schuster), and the Broadway hit, *A Thurber Carnival*.